LIFE IN A GARDEN

ACTIVITIES AND PROJECTS FOR THE OUTDOOR CLASSROOM,

YEARS F-6

ROSS MARS

© 2023 Ross Mars

All rights reserved. No part of this book may be reproduced or transmitted in any form or by any means, electronic or mechanical, including photocopying, recording or by any information storage and retrieval system, without prior permission in writing from the publisher.

Reproducible on pages 11-14, 20-21, 29, 35, 37, 44, 49, 50, 62, 69-70, 94-96, 100, 103-104, 108-109

Access the resources, templates and reproducibles from the book at
www.ambapress.com.au/products/life-in-a-garden

Published in 2023 by Amba Press, Melbourne, Australia.
www.ambapress.com.au

Previously published in 2020 by Hawker Brownlow Education.

This edition replaces all previous editions.

ISBN: 9781923116160 (pbk)
ISBN: 9781923116177 (ebk)

A catalogue record for this book is available from the National Library of Australia.

Illustrations by Brenna Quinlan, Simone Willis, Leanne White
Photography by istock, Freepik, Pixabay, Pexels, Wikimedia

ACKNOWLEDGEMENTS

My sincere thanks go to Brenna Quinlan, Simone Willis and Leanne White for their artwork and drawings and to Jenny for her continued support and encouragement.

CONTENTS

About the author vii

PART 1: INTRODUCING THE OUTDOOR CLASSROOM 1

Teacher's notes: Designing your school garden 2
Teacher's notes: Building garden beds 6
Teacher's notes: Planting strategies 8
Gardening skills: Safety in the outdoor classroom 10
Project: Exploring the garden 11
Gardening skills: Gardening tools 15

PART 2: HEALTHY SOIL, HEALTHY PLANTS 17

Investigation: What do plants need? 18
Teacher's notes: Soil 22
Investigation: Soil particles 23
Investigation: Soil permeability 24
Investigation: More soil activities 26
Teacher's notes: Earthworms 27
Project: Earthworms in action! 29
Gardening skills: Composting 30
Investigation: Banana breakdown 32
Teacher's notes: Mulch 33
Investigation: Evaporation 34
Investigation: Comparing mulches 36
Gardening skills: Testing soil moisture and watering plants 38

PART 3: FROM SEED TO PLANT AND BACK AGAIN 41

Teacher's notes: Seeds 42
Investigation: What's inside a seed? 43
Gardening skills: Planting seeds 45
Teacher's notes: Seed germination 51
Investigation: Germination in a jar 52
Project: Mini hothouses 53
Project: Terrariums 54
Investigation: Stems and leaves 56
Teacher's notes: Flowers and pollination 58
Project: Make a butterfly feeder 60

Project: Make a bee hotel 63
Gardening skills: Harvesting garden vegetables and fruit 64
Investigation: Fruit sorting 67
Project: Make products from herbs 71
Project: Preserving food 77
Project: Recipes for excess garden produce 80
Gardening skills: Collecting seed from the garden 84
Gardening skills: Seed bombs 85
Gardening skills: Resprouting vegetables 86

PART 4: THE GARDEN ENVIRONMENT 87

Teacher's notes: Observing life cycles in the garden 88
Teacher's notes: Interactions in the garden 91
Investigation: Animal interactions simulation 92
Teacher's notes: Adaptations in the garden 97
Investigation: Observing adaptations of climbing plants 98
Teacher's notes: Seed dispersal 101
Investigation: Design a seed 102
Gardening skills: Pest management 105
Project: Make a fruit fly trap 108
Teacher's notes: Seasons and change 110
Investigation: Hidden colours 111
Project: Exploring plant dyes 113

APPENDIX 117

Planting guide 117
Vegetables and garden salad fruits for winter 118
Vegetables and garden salad fruits for summer 120
Herbs 122
Native plants 124
Bush medicine plants 128
Plants for attracting butterflies 130
Plants for attracting other beneficial insects 132
Australian Curriculum alignment 134
Planting diary template 138
Answer sheet 140

ABOUT THE AUTHOR

Dr Ross Mars began his career as a senior high school science teacher, writing and co-writing a number of books about science and technology.

Over the last 20 years he has worked in the water industry, focusing on wastewater treatment and reuse, and has presented papers at a number of international conferences, both in Australia and overseas, and has had several papers published in scientific journals.

Ross is one of the most authoritative permaculture teachers, designers and consultants in Australia, and author of three books on the subject as well as other resources on energy-efficient housing design and renewable energy systems for power generation. He has a strong interest in preparing people for the transition to sustainable living, especially as we move into a challenging and uncertain future.

More recently, Ross has developed and introduced the new Accredited Permaculture courses in Western Australia, including Certificate I and Certificate II VET programs for schools and community groups as well as a Diploma of Permaculture. He continues as an educator and an author.

PART 1
INTRODUCING THE OUTDOOR CLASSROOM

What better place is there for students to become partners with the natural world than a school garden? Creating an 'outdoor classroom' is the perfect way for students to explore and contribute to a thriving ecosystem of interesting plants and animals.

This section includes a handy guide for building or improving your school garden, as well as some simple ways to introduce your students to the garden environment.

TEACHER'S NOTES:
Designing your school garden 2
Building garden beds 6
Planting strategies 8

PROJECTS:
Exploring the garden 11

GARDENING SKILLS:
Safety in the outdoor classroom 10
Using tools in the garden 15

Teacher's Notes

Designing Your School Garden

Whether you are involved in starting a school garden from scratch, or are simply looking to improve an existing one, the following pages will offer some useful strategies that will help you get the most out of your experience.

Conducting a Needs Analysis

Schools present a unique challenge when it comes to garden design. For one thing, nobody lives there; students grow up and leave each year, and teachers who were once heavily involved in promoting and maintaining the garden eventually move on to new schools. Some gardens may also be more vulnerable to vandalism or invasion from animals. It's therefore a necessity to conduct a thorough analysis of the needs and capacity of the school to build and maintain a garden.

The School Community

To determine the needs and level of support in the school community, you should discuss your ideas with a wide variety of people. This should include the teachers who want to use the area, your principal and administrators, the gardener and maintenance staff, and members of the school council or parents and friends association.

The Potential Site

Planning a new garden requires a realistic assessment of what is possible. The development of the school grounds should be in line with the vision for the future direction of the school. Many schools already have a master grounds plan, so your design needs to complement any existing school plans. Survey the area, noting any existing structures and amenities such as easy access to water sources etc. Auditing the site for positive and negative features can help to manage expectations and avoid discouragement when things don't go to plan.

The Budget

As with any large project, budget limitations are often the biggest stumbling block for the development of a school garden. Even when school administration and staff are generally supportive, a lack of resources can often dampen initial enthusiasm. If money is an issue, the local community may be able to assist. Gardening materials can be obtained from a variety of sources, such as donations from local nurseries and landscape suppliers. You may wish to hold a tool and supply donation drive, which can also spark awareness and interest among the school community.

Determining Resources

Accessing resources and materials is an ongoing project that needs to be considered in the initial design stages. Beyond budget constraints, resources can take the form of people, materials and energy. Securing 'people resources' should be a high priority. Individual teachers don't have time to spend maintaining the garden, so this responsibility must be shared. Staff training and professional development is crucial to the success of a school garden area. At the very least, the school should make a financial and supportive commitment to make sure several staff have an active interest in the garden.

Teacher's Notes

Having a school gardener who is sympathetic to the outdoor classroom ideas is an added bonus for any school. But schools that do not have a regular gardener may not have to look far. Many parents and members of the wider community are often willing to devote some regular time and energy to maintaining the school garden.

Some Guidelines for Designing School Gardens

Once you have conducted your needs analysis, it's time to begin designing your garden. Here are some useful guidelines when considering building or making improvements to your garden:

- Involve children as much as you can. Show them how to build sheet mulch garden beds, visit established local properties and discuss the main principles and concepts of sustainable living. Many students will begin to understand these ideas when they can see how they are connected to the ongoing health of the garden environment.

- It may not be possible for the students to come up with a fully functioning design for the garden, but unless they have some ownership of the plan the future success of the garden area is not guaranteed. Children get excited and willing to work when they know that what they are doing is something they have contributed to. You may be surprised at the number of really good (and innovative) suggestions they make about the garden and site development. Lead them gently through the process.

- Consider the needs of the children. Small areas are great for young children, but not so much for older students. Garden beds may have to be smaller than usual so that children can access all areas easily.

- Some gardens are large enough to enable each class to care for their own garden bed. Where this is not possible, consider building small garden areas nearby each classroom, rather than one larger area away from the school.

- Involving specialist teachers can help extend the sense of ownership among staff and students. For example, an art teacher may have students create garden sculptures, or functional features such as bird baths.

- Gardening allows students to see the connection between what they are growing and the food they eat at home. It's worth considering how garden produce will be distributed. Will students be able to take fruit and vegetables home? Can you donate

TEACHER'S NOTES

food to the school canteen? Can you sell items at the school fete, or run events like a mini farmer's market, with proceeds going towards garden maintenance or charitable causes?

- Some garden beds could contain plants for propagation work. These stock garden beds may contain small beds of particular herbs that are used for cuttings and grafting work. Beds could have different themes. For example, one bed for culinary herbs, another for medicinal herbs and another for pest-repellent herbs. Students could then take small pieces of these plants from the stock beds for their own use.

- The outdoor classroom presents an array of opportunities for scientific observation. You'll be surprised what you will attract by simply adding some nesting boxes, bird baths or feeding trays. Try building a weather station that holds equipment which measures daily temperature and barometer changes, humidity, rainfall and wind direction and speed.

Teacher's Notes

Practical Design Considerations

The number of activities, garden ideas and design strategies are endless. Teachers and students will be able to experiment and see what works best for them. Here are a few ideas and practical considerations that have worked well in schools:

- **Consider your storage options:** Where will tools such as shovels, pitchforks, hand trowels, gloves and wheelbarrows be stored? What about potting mix, plant pots, watering cans and seeds? Can you put a lockable shed in the design so that all of these are available on site?

- **Plan for space:** Ensure that your garden can easily accommodate an average class. Consider bench seats and areas of lawn where students can sit and work. Not everybody has to work on the garden beds during the lesson. Some will want to plan, record, draw and think.

- **Pathways:** A pathway about 1.2 metres wide is ample for school gardens. Smaller pathways are more suitable for individual (student) garden areas, or to lead to quiet places within the garden. As a rule of thumb, plan for a couple of students walking side-by-side or for a wheelbarrow to pass through with some leeway to avoid accidents.

- **A secret garden area:** Secluded garden areas provide sanctuary. It is possible to include areas for student privacy, yet still make these visible to teachers.

- **Simple log or bench seats:** Provide spaces for students to sit and talk or to eat their lunch. Rock or carved seats can really look great.

- **Shaded areas:** Plan for some areas to be shaded. These spaces can be much more inviting than areas in direct sunlight. This could mean placing some seats under large trees or using structures like arbours and pergolas.

- **Nursery:** Developing your own shrub and tree nursery will help in reducing costs of obtaining plant stock for the garden. This can be as simple as a potting area, a small shade-house (covered frame) or a series of benches in a hothouse for plant propagation.

- **Compost:** Be mindful of where you place your compost area. Freshly made compost tends to smell, especially when you use animal manures. It's best to place this area away from buildings, but with easy access to the garden.

PART I

Teacher's Notes

Building Garden Beds

There are a great many ways to build garden beds in schools. You don't have to buy expensive, steel raised garden beds to grow food: vegetables and herbs can be planted directly into the ground, provided that the soil is prepared properly. Soil fertility can be improved with mulches, manures, green manure crops and other organic matter.

Adding borders to your garden beds is essential for containing the soil and defining the area where plants are grown and maintained. Borders can be made from rocks, limestone blocks, sleepers, bricks and even straw bales. These materials are easily sourced and relatively cheap, or even free with a few community connections.

Most garden beds are built up a little so that plants are growing in plenty of good soil. The beds should be at least 30 centimetres high for growing most vegetables. This allows beds to be placed on concrete or paving. Steel sheeting can make for an ideal raised garden bed. Some sheeting products are able to be curved and formed into various shapes. Normal corrugated steel roof-sheeting is thinner and unable to be curved, but can still be used in rectangular or square-shaped beds. Be sure to add posts on the corners to secure each side.

Teacher's Notes

These illustrations highlight that there are many different ways you might set up your own garden bed. Your choice may depend on the available space, the quality of the soil or your access to materials.

Straw bales make great garden beds or structures for maintaining a compost pile. You can either make a shape with them and fill them with a mixture of sand and compost or scoop out the middle of the bale, fill with soil and plant directly into it. Eventually the straw bales break down, at which point you can put all of this organic matter into the compost bin, and start all over again for the next season's crops.

When filling garden beds, try to use good soil. Generally, plants only require soils with 5 per cent organic matter, so pure compost can be 'diluted' and vegetables will still grow well. Add some sand to your compost to create an ideal growing medium.

Soil with good levels of organic matter will result in both higher water retention in the soil and increased water availability to the plants. Don't forget to add mulch once the garden beds are set up, as this helps reduce weeds, keeps the soil cool and traps moisture. The mulch also increases the organic content and biological activity of the soil as it breaks down.

PART 1

Teacher's Notes

PLANTING STRATEGIES

There is no magic formula for positioning vegetables in a garden bed, but some general strategies can keep plants thriving and productive.

CROP ROTATION

Crop rotation is a traditional organic planting practice that involves planting a different food crop in the same area each year, using five to six year cycles. Each plant contributes to the soil in different ways, which can benefit the following year's crop. For example, foods in the *Brassica* family (broccoli, cauliflower and cabbage) are nutrient-hungry and they can quickly deplete stocks of nitrogen from the soil. The next year, it would be best to plant a leguminous crop (such as peas or beans), which replenishes nitrogen over time.

Rotating crops also helps to minimise pest problems in the soil. A pest that prefers one type of crop will be deprived of their food source the following year, thereby interrupting their life cycles and keeping populations to a minimum.

Although certain crops can benefit the soil in different ways, manually adding nutrients is still essential. Topping up the soil with plenty of compost and other natural fertilisers before planting each season ensures that crops remain healthy and productive. The practice of resting the soil (becoming 'fallow') by planting a green manure crop or a legume (or something that is both) is also worthwhile to rebuild soil fertility.

Teacher's Notes

Permaculture Planting

Unlike crop rotation, permaculture planting is an integrated style of garden in which a variety of plants share the same bed. Vegetables aren't planted in rows but scattered throughout.

Permaculture makes use of 'companion planting' and other techniques to mask the shape, colour and smell of vegetables so pests cannot easily find them. It's also possible to squeeze the plants a little closer than normal through a process called 'stacking'. Here, plants are layered in such a way that they can all receive sunlight, but those that require some shade are protected. In the image above, you will notice the pea climbing up a corn plant. There is also a general decrease in height from left to right – as plants face towards the sun.

The permaculture approach allows for some creativity in plant placement, but here are some handy hints to consider:

- Tall crops, such as corn, tomatoes and climbing plants (peas, beans), should be planted on the southern side of the bed. These will not shade out smaller plants in front.
- Climbing plants like peas, beans and tomatoes need support. Build a simple structure or trellis to help keep them upright.
- Consider the anticipated size (height and width) of the plant so that you can space them apart appropriately.
- Think about how long certain vegetables take to mature before you can harvest them. Plant brassicas throughout a garden bed and then onions or garlic along with lettuces and radishes between them. By the time you harvest the onions and garlic, you would have already picked radish, lettuce and then broccoli.
- Make sure that you top up the garden beds after each harvest with good soil, full of compost and organic matter.

GARDENING SKILLS

SAFETY IN THE OUTDOOR CLASSROOM

It is important to model correct behaviour in the garden. This short activity will help younger students understand the school garden as an extension of the classroom and introduce them to the rules they will need to follow while spending time there.

MATERIALS

- ☑ materials for making posters
- ☑ laminating equipment
- ☑ garden stakes

METHOD

1. In the classroom, speak with students about the school garden. What can they expect to find there? *Plants, garden beds, flowers, pathways, benches etc.*

2. Explain that the garden is like an outdoor classroom. This means that we must follow the classroom rules, and also add some new ones especially for this area. These rules help to keep us safe while working outdoors.

3. Display some of the classroom rules on the board, including those that may not apply to the garden. Discuss which rules should still apply and erase those that do not.

4. Ask students whether they can think of any things they should wear in the garden. *Gloves, hat, sunscreen, closed-toed shoes or other personal protective clothing.*

5. Take the class into the garden to point out some of its features. Point out visual markers that determine the boundaries of the 'outdoor classroom'. If the boundaries are difficult to determine, you might want to use witches hats or coloured markers. Ask students to think about some of the safety issues they see in the garden, so that when they return to class they can write some rules to follow when they are working outside.

6. Upon returning to the classroom, ask students if they can think of any other rules that might need to be added. Have them practise phrasing their rules positively, e.g. *'Walk along the paths'*, not *'Don't run'*.

7. Have students design signs illustrating one rule to be followed in the garden. Laminate these and attach them to garden stakes. These signs can then be placed in the garden bed as a visual reminder for students while you work with them in the garden. For a greater effect, have students bring the completed signs with them every time they go to the garden, and take them back when your time in the garden is over. It may be helpful to have students reflect on whether they were able to follow the garden rules after their first few sessions in the garden.

PROJECT
EXPLORING THE GARDEN

PART 1

This activity will allow students to familiarise themselves with the garden and its features, while considering the design considerations that go into building a garden.

MATERIALS

- ☑ activity sheet: a garden audit
- ☑ activity sheet: design a garden
- ☑ measuring equipment (metre rulers, measuring tape, trundle wheels etc.)

METHOD

1. Allow students to explore the garden, taking note of the garden's features using the activity sheet *A garden audit* on page 12. Students should use measuring equipment to gauge the size of garden beds, paths etc.

2. Upon returning to the classroom, discuss what students have discovered. As they share their findings, ask students questions about the garden's design. For example, 'Why do you think some garden beds are larger than others? Should the paths be wider? Why is it important for the compost to be further away from the garden?'

3. Tell students that they will be using what they have discussed to design their own garden. Students can use either the worksheet on page 14, some A4 graph paper or even an A3 poster. Several online tools are also available, such as the one found here: https://www.gardena.com/uk/garden-life/garden-planner/

4. To challenge older students, some constraints should be added.

    Some examples of constraints may include:
    - ☑ The garden must include eight garden beds.
    - ☑ There should be at least 60 metres of path.
    - ☑ The garden needs two water sources.
    - ☑ There must be at least three areas for people to sit.

5. Students should have the opportunity to present their designs to the class, explaining some of the design decisions they have made.

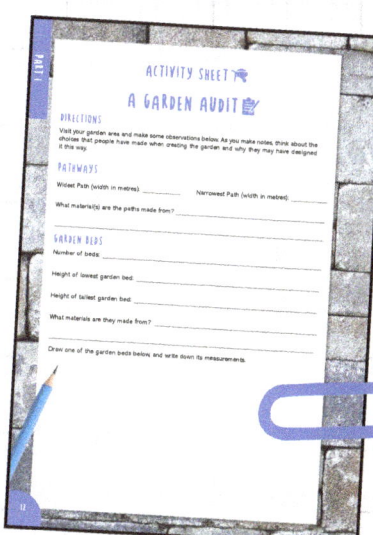

PART 1

ACTIVITY SHEET
A GARDEN AUDIT

DIRECTIONS
Visit your garden area and make some observations below. As you make notes, think about the choices that people have made when creating the garden and why they may have designed it this way.

PATHWAYS

Widest path (width in metres): _____   Narrowest path (width in metres): _____

What material(s) are the paths made from? _____
_____

GARDEN BEDS

Number of beds: _____

Height of lowest garden bed: _____

Height of tallest garden bed: _____

What materials are they made from? _____
_____

Draw one of the garden beds below, and write down its measurements.

ACTIVITY SHEET

A GARDEN AUDIT

TICK THE APPROPRIATE BOX:

WASTE MANAGEMENT

Item	Yes	No
Compost bays (large)		
Compost bin (smaller)		
Earthworm farm		
Chickens or other animals		

What is the main way organic material is recycled?

_____

WATER SOURCES

Item	Yes	No
Tap (mains)		
Pond		
Rainwater tank		
Bore irrigation		
Mains water irrigation		
Greywater reuse		
Hand watering		

What are some advantages of using rainwater tanks?

_____

UTILITIES AND STRUCTURES

Which of these can be found in your garden?

Item	Yes	No
Toolshed or enclosure		
Flower pots		
Potting bench		
Garden seats		
BBQ or pizza oven		

Item	Yes	No
Gazebo		
Trellis		
Quiet space/area		
Nursery/propagation area		
Shadehouse/hothouse		

PLANTS

List examples of the following plants you find in the garden.

Large, shady trees: _____

Herbs: _____

Fruits and vegetables: _____

Other plants: _____

_____

_____

PART 1

PART 1

ACTIVITY SHEET
DESIGN A GARDEN

DIRECTIONS

Use the grid to create a birds-eye view diagram of your very own garden. Remember to add a scale at the bottom of the grid to show the actual size of objects on the map

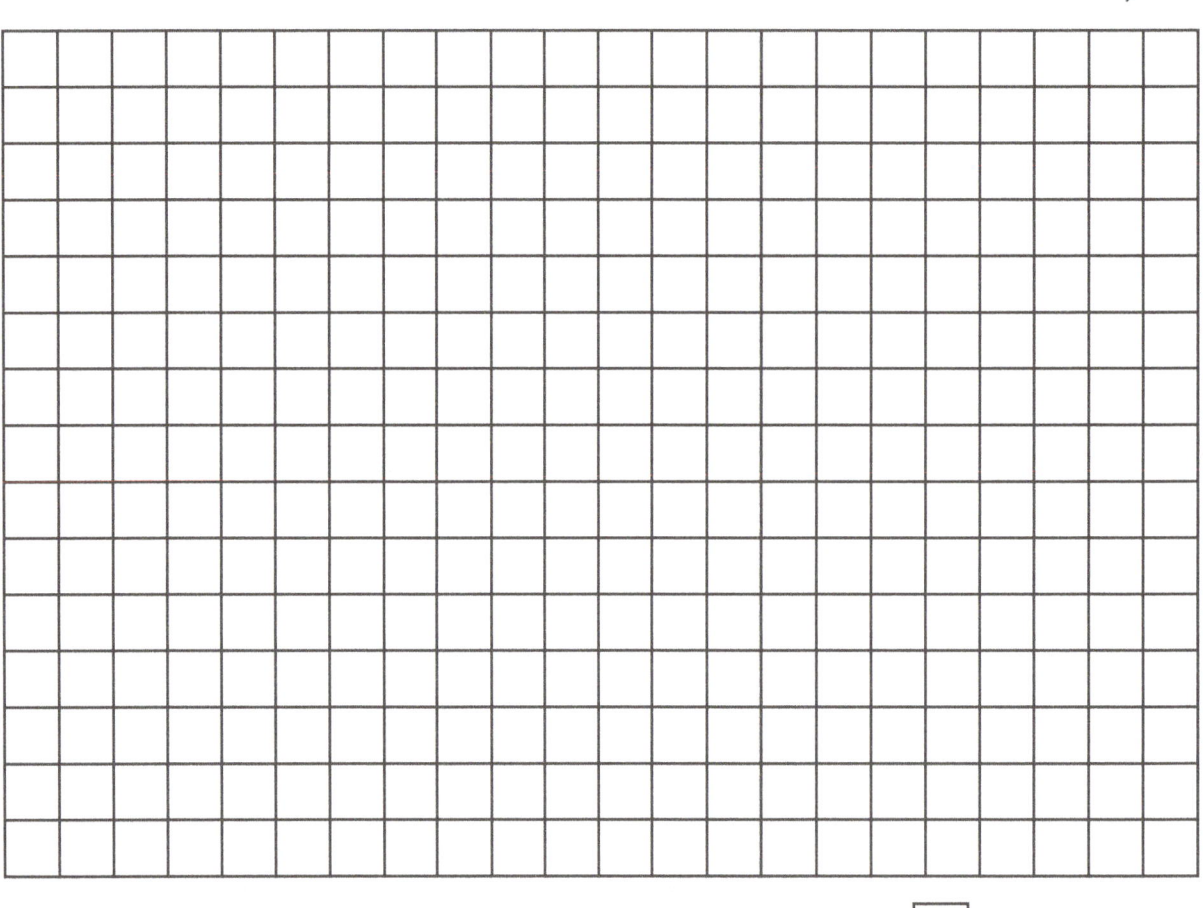

☐ = _____ m²

Describe some of the features of your garden and why you have chosen to design it this way.

_____
_____
_____
_____
_____
_____
_____

GARDENING SKILLS

GARDENING TOOLS

The following simple activities are designed for younger students to get to know and practise with some of the tools used in the garden.

MYSTERY TOOLS

MATERIALS

- ☑ common gardening tools for display (e.g. shovel, spade, leaf rake, metal rake, weeding fork, hand fork, shears, pruning shears, mulch fork, hand trowel)
- ☑ pieces of cloth, enough to cover the head of each tool
- ☑ wheelbarrow to carry tools back to storage area

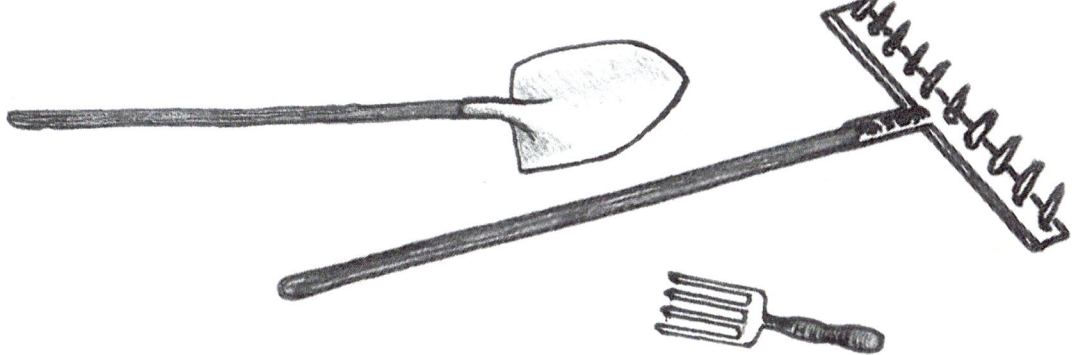

SET-UP

Wrap the ends of each tool with cloth, leaving the handles exposed. This activity is designed to take place in the garden area but can easily be adapted for the classroom.

METHOD

1. Take students to the area where you have set up the equipment. Tell students that they will be looking at some useful tools that they might use in the garden.

2. Present a tool and have students examine the exposed features and general size to guess what kind of tool it might be: e.g. *'This one has two handles'*, *'This one is larger than the others'* or *'This one has a long, wooden handle'*.

3. Ask one student to carefully remove the cloth from the tool. Discuss the tool with the students, including its name, and what it is used for. You may also like to bring up any safety issues that need to be discussed.

4. Ask another student to take the tool and place it in the wheelbarrow to be taken away once all tools have been unwrapped.

Continued...

PART 1

PART 1

GARDENING SKILLS

GARDENING TOOLS

USING TOOLS

MATERIALS:

☑ hand trowels or weeding forks, enough for at least one per pair of students

METHOD

1. Take students outside and tell them that they are going to practise using some of these tools to do an important job: weeding the garden.

2. Ask students if they know what a 'weed' is. Guide students to understand that a weed is a plant that grows in a place where it is not wanted. Weeds grow very quickly in a garden and use up the water and food that is meant for other plants. Point out some weeds in the garden bed to show the difference between unwanted plants and those that belong there.

3. Using a hand trowel or weeding fork, demonstrate to students how to dig around a weed before pulling it up and disposing of it appropriately. Review appropriate safety rules before handing out a trowel or fork to pairs of students and have them practise weeding.

PART 2
HEALTHY SOIL, HEALTHY PLANTS

Soil is much more than sand and leaf litter. It's a complex mixture of physical, chemical and biological components, all of which contribute to the health of the plants and other soil-based life. Soil health and quality are the keys to sustainable agriculture. Healthy soil makes healthy plants, and healthy plants make healthy people!

The activities in this section help students understand how soil provides for the needs of plants, and how we can maintain soil quality to ensure a thriving and productive garden.

TEACHER'S NOTES:

Soil	22
Earthworms	27
Mulch	33

PROJECTS:

Earthworms in action!	29

GARDENING SKILLS:

Composting	30
Testing moisture and watering plants	38

INVESTIGATIONS:

What do plants need?	18
Soil particles	23
Soil permeability	24
More soil activities	26
Banana breakdown	32
Evaporation	34
Comparing mulches	36

INVESTIGATION

WHAT DO PLANTS NEED?

This investigation will help students understand that plants are living organisms, which rely on specific conditions for their continued growth and survival. Students will compare healthy seedlings with those that are deprived of their basic needs.

PART 2

MATERIALS

- ☑ paper cups – cut down to about 4 cm high
- ☑ sprouts or small seedlings
- ☑ potting mix, containing compost (this is required to supply nutrients to plants)
- ☑ water, teaspoon to measure volume
- ☑ activated charcoal
- ☑ refrigerator or small esky with ice packs
- ☑ textas
- ☑ activity cards (page 20; copy and cut out)

SET-UP

For this activity, you can either purchase sprouts or generate your own by placing peas, mung beans, wheat or corn seeds on some saturated cotton wool in a saucer or shallow dish. Place in a cupboard and keep moist. The seeds should sprout within a week or two.

BACKGROUND NOTES

SUNLIGHT

Sunlight is crucial for plants to grow and survive. Sunlight is required in the process of photosynthesis where sugars and other substances are produced.

WATER

All living things require water. Water is needed for all cell reactions and to transport materials throughout the plant.

NUTRITION

Minerals found in the soil provide the essential nutrients that all organisms need to enable chemical reactions and for general health and wellbeing.

INVESTIGATION

WARMTH

The temperature affects the speed of reactions in a cell. Enzymes work within a specific temperature range, so if it is too hot or too cold the organism doesn't function at an optimum level.

AIR

Plants need two gases from the air – oxygen and carbon dioxide. Oxygen is required for respiration, while carbon dioxide is required for the process of photosynthesis.

To ensure gases are removed (or at least minimised) you need to use a substance that primarily absorbs carbon dioxide. This is the role of the activated charcoal in the experiment.

METHOD

1. Brainstorm with students about the things that human beings need to live and grow. *Food, water, sleep, oxygen,* etc.

2. Ask students, 'Are plants living things? How do you know? What do you think plants need to live and grow?' As you receive suggestions, make a table or Venn diagram on the board comparing the needs of human beings with those of plants.

3. Guide students to understand that plants require nutrition, sunlight, the right temperature, water and air.

4. Share with students that they will be conducting an experiment to see what might happen to a plant when they don't get everything they need to stay healthy.

5. Divide students into groups of three or four and distribute two seedlings, potting mix, water, markers and teaspoons to each group. One group will need the activated charcoal.

6. Copy and cut out the activity cards. Give one of the five activity cards to each group. Each activity will produce one healthy seedling and one that is deprived of either sunlight, water, soil, warmth or air. Ideally, the one kept outside should be protected from wind and rain, but still be able to have sunlight falling on it. Check the moisture of the soil and add small amounts of water to keep it moist as the plants grow.

7. Students will track the results over a couple of weeks (you may wish to use the planting diary on page 138 for this). Changes should be evident by then, but extend the activity a little longer if required.

8. Discuss findings with your students. Some questions for reflection include:

   - What similarities or differences do you see among the seedlings?
   - Why is it important to know what plants need?
   - How might knowing how plants react when they are deprived of certain needs be helpful when we're working with plants in the garden?

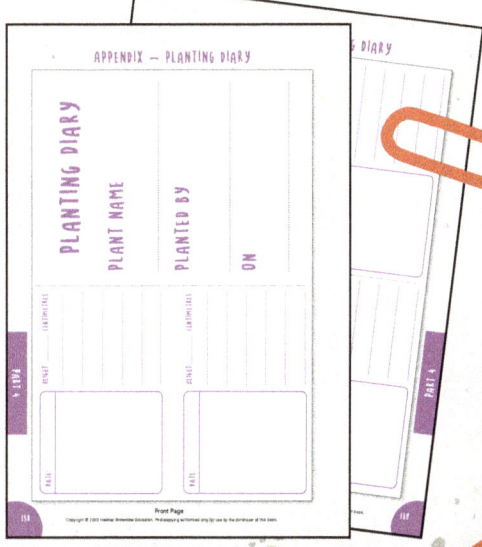

ACTIVITY SHEET
ACTIVITY CARDS: WHAT DO PLANTS NEED?

PART 2

SUNLIGHT

1. Place one seedling in each cup. Cover it with 1 cm of soil.
2. Add one or two teaspoons of water to each cup.
3. Use a texta to label one cup 'sunlight' and the other 'no sunlight'.
4. Place the 'sunlight' cup in a sunny spot, like a classroom window sill or somewhere outside.
5. Place the 'no sunlight' cup in a dark cupboard.
6. Add water to the cups over the next two weeks.

NUTRITION

1. Place one seedling in each cup.
2. Add 1 cm of soil to **one cup only**. Do not place any soil in the other cup.
3. Add one or two teaspoons of water to each cup.
4. Use a texta to label the cup with 'soil' and the other 'no soil'.
5. Place both cups in a sunny spot, like a classroom window sill or somewhere outside.
6. Add water to the cups over the next two weeks.

ACTIVITY SHEET

WATER

1. Place one seedling in each cup. Cover it with 1 cm of soil.
2. Add one or two teaspoons of water to only one cup.
3. Use a texta to label one cup 'water' and the other 'no water'.
4. Place both cups in a sunny spot, like a classroom window sill or somewhere outside.
5. Add water to the 'water' cup over the next two weeks.

TEMPERATURE

1. Place one seedling in each cup. Cover both with 1 cm of soil.
2. Add one or two teaspoons of water to both cups.
3. Use a texta to label one cup 'warm' and the other 'cold'.
4. Place the 'warm' cup on a classroom shelf that doesn't receive direct sunlight. Place the 'cold' cup in a refrigerator or an esky which is kept cold with an ice pack.
5. Add water as needed to both cups over the next two weeks.

AIR

1. Place one seedling in each cup. Cover it with 1 cm of soil.
2. Add one or two teaspoons of water to both cups.
3. Use a texta to label one cup 'air' and the other 'no air'.
4. Place the 'no air' cup in a zip-lock bag. Add one teaspoon of activated charcoal to the bag (not in the cup). Zip the bag about half way, then squeeze as much air as you can out of the bag. Close the bag completely.
5. Place both cups in a sunny spot, like a classroom window sill or somewhere outside.
6. Add water to the cups over the next two weeks.

PART 2

TEACHER'S NOTES

SOIL

Soil provides much of what plants require for healthy growth. **Minerals** found in the soil provide the essential nutrients that all organisms need to make products, enable reactions to proceed and for general health and wellbeing. **Water** is essential for transporting nutrients from the soil to the plant. It is also an essential ingredient for photosynthesis, which allows the plant to produce food for itself in the form of glucose. **Air spaces in soil** allow room for plants to breathe and grow – when soil is too compacted, roots cannot spread through the soil, and the plant is unable to anchor itself to the ground.

SOIL COMPOSITION

Soil generally consists of a mixture of several particles. **Sand** is by far the largest particle. Its size allows pockets of air to be trapped throughout the soil, which also provides effective water drainage to prevent roots from being damaged. The much finer particles of **silt** and **clay** often fill these gaps, which helps retain water and keep it from draining away too quickly for the plants to use.

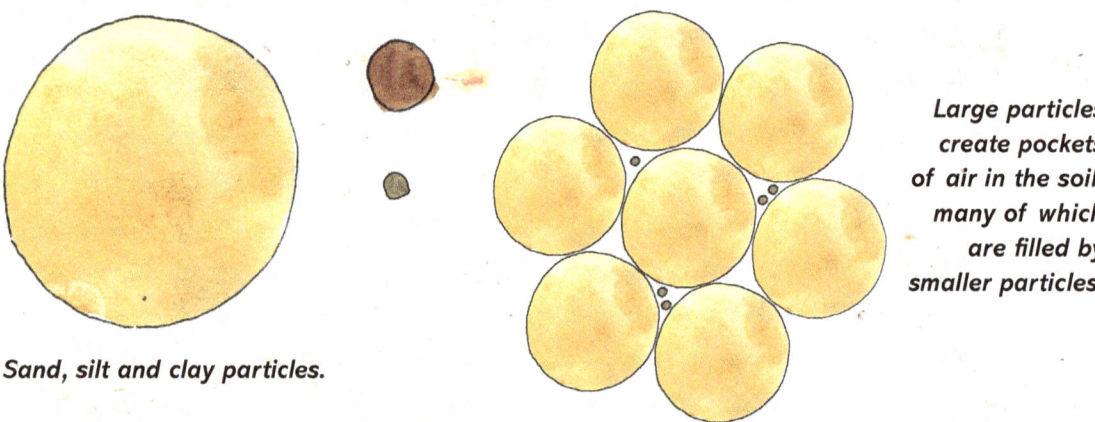

Sand, silt and clay particles.

Large particles create pockets of air in the soil, many of which are filled by smaller particles.

HUMUS

Humus is remnants of decomposed organic matter. It is slowly broken down by creatures in the soil, releasing the nutrients held within it. Humus can also help create pockets of air, while its sponge-like structure can also retain water.

LOAM

The amounts of soil particles, humus, water and organisms vary widely from location to location, and all of these can be combined to produce a wide range of different soils. Many plants have adapted to thrive in soil of every ratio, from predominantly sand to mostly clay, but we tend to grow our edible crops in a mixture of soil particles we call loam. Loam is that mixture of clay, silt and sand that seems to have the best properties for growing vegetables – enough clay and silt to hold water, and enough sand to provide space for air and prevent waterlogging. Add some organic matter (up to 5 per cent is adequate) and you have the perfect soil for growing food.

KEEPING SOIL PRODUCTIVE

Since plants take up the nutrients from the soil, we need to develop strategies to replace lost fertility. This is why gardeners must add compost, manures and other amendments to rebuild the soil ready for next season's food crop. Rotating crops also allows different types of plants to re-aerate the soil and re-introduce organic matter to build healthy soil once again.

INVESTIGATION

SOIL PARTICLES

In this simple activity, students will observe the composition of a soil sample by separating its particles into layers.

MATERIALS

- ☑ 100 ml tall glass jar or plastic bottle with stopper or lid
- ☑ hand trowels, one for each group
- ☑ funnel
- ☑ textas and masking tape for labelling

METHOD

1. Ask students, if there is a difference between soil and dirt. Guide them to understand that soil contains minerals, air and water, all of which supports the life of plants and other living things that live inside the soil. Dirt is composed mostly of soil particles, and does not contain any nutrients or water for the plant.

2. Explain that soil is made of several different particles: sand, silt and clay, which help distribute water, air and nutrients to the plant. Sand particles are large, while silt and clay particles are much smaller. Organic matter such as leaf litter and compost is also an important component. It provides nutrients for the soil as it breaks down. Small particles of broken-down organic matter is called humus.

3. Divide students into groups and provide them with a jar or bottle with a lid. Have them choose an area of the school grounds with a plant close by. Using a trowel, they can take a sample of soil, filling their jar to around half way using a funnel (a piece of paper rolled into a funnel shape will suffice).

4. Students should label their bottle using the masking tape and textas, indicating where the soil came from and what kind of plants were nearby. They can also perform the ribbon test (see page 26) to make predictions of their sample's composition.

5. Students should then fill their jar with water, screw on the lid and shake vigorously for 10–20 seconds. Allow the water to settle in a spot where students can make observations over time. The water eventually becomes clearer and layers of different-sized particles can be seen. As the soil settles, students may even notice air bubbles coming out of the soil.

6. Have students identify the particles contained in their soil sample. The particles that settle on the bottom will be sand, while those resting on top of the sand (or floating below the surface of the water) will be clay and silt. Humus will be floating on top of the water.

7. Students may then check their predictions about the composition of their soil sample, and compare their sample with those from other locations.

8. Discuss results with students. Some questions for reflection include:
   - Did all soil samples have the same amount of sand, clay, silt or humus?
   - What can this tell us about the needs of different plants?

INVESTIGATION

SOIL PERMEABILITY

This experiment allows students to visualise the role of various soil particles in transporting and retaining air, water and nutrients to sustain plants and other soil-based life.

PART 2

MATERIALS

- ☑ several large jars or drinking glasses
- ☑ 3–4 golf balls
- ☑ bag of marbles
- ☑ collection of small beads (smaller than the marbles)
- ☑ funnels
- ☑ graded measuring cups
- ☑ stopwatches
- ☑ filter paper or paper towel
- ☑ samples of soil: sandy soil, clayey soil and loam. (If you cannot access clay or loam, plain sand mixed with some bagged garden soil will suffice.) Each sample should contain around the same amount of soil – enough to fill a funnel to at least three-quarters.

SET-UP

Place golf balls, marbles and beads into three separate jars. Line a funnel with filter paper.

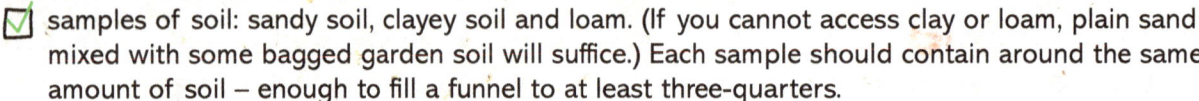

24

INVESTIGATION

METHOD

1. Show students the three jars containing golf balls, marbles and beads. Ask students whether or not the jars are full. Guide them to understand that, although the jars are full of balls and beads, there are still gaps of air inside. Which jar seems to have the most space? Which one has the least?

2. Remind students that soil particles have differing sizes (see notes on page 22). Have students identify what kind of particle each ball might represent. Explain that soil is **porous** – it contains gaps for air and water to move through. The ability for air and soil to move through soil is called **permeability**.

3. Remove the golf balls from their jar. Place them in the funnel and then rest the funnel in the jar. Have one student use a measuring cup to pour about a cup of water into the funnel, while another uses the stopwatch to time how long the water takes to drain into the jar.

4. Add some marbles and beads to the funnel. Move the contents around slightly so that they fill the gaps between the golf balls, then repeat the experiment with the water. The water should take longer to drain this time. Have students suggest reasons for why this might be. (Larger gaps between the golf balls allow water to drain away more easily, but the beads and marbles plug some of these gaps so that water is retained for longer.)

5. Explain that it is important for soil to hold on to water so that plants can access it, but too much water can deprive the plant of air, and also damage the roots. Most plants grow best in soil that can provide both air and water, but excess water must be able to drain away. Larger particles like sand provide air and drainage. Smaller particles help soil retain water and nutrients for longer, but do not provide a lot of air, or space for the plant's roots to spread.

6. Hand a jar, funnel, soil sample and filter paper to each group of students. Have them rest the funnel in their jar, line it with filter paper and add their soil sample. (Alternative equipment and set-ups appear in the images below.)

7. Use a measuring cup to add a cup of water to the top of the soil. Have one student use a stopwatch to time how long the majority of the water takes to collect in the jar below. Measure the water that has passed through so that students can determine how much water had been held by the soil.

8. Once students have collected their data, they can draw conclusions about the composition of their soil sample and discuss their findings with the class. Reveal the composition of each soil sample so that students can see whether they were correct.

INVESTIGATION

MORE SOIL ACTIVITIES

RIBBON TEST FOR SOILS

This is a simple activity to help students guess the composition of soil based on texture. Sandy soil feels very gritty while clayey soil is smooth. The ribbon test is performed by adding a small amount of water to a dessert spoon of soil to make a ball. You need to be able to roll it and mix the water into the soil.

Squeeze the soil out between your thumb and forefinger to make a thin 'ribbon'. Measure the length of the ribbon before it falls from your hand. Repeat a few times to get an average length of ribbon. Sandy soils fall apart at less than 10 millimetres, loam about 20–30 millimetres while clay can be 70 millimetres or more. Various combinations of soil particles fall within this range.

Students can be encouraged to make predictions about the composition of various soils they have access to.

TESTING FOR WATER REPELLENCY IN SOILS

Many Australian soils suffer from water repellency. When water is added to a soil it runs off without soaking in. This is due to degrading plant matter creating a waxy coating on the soil grains, which causes water to roll away just like it would do on greaseproof paper.

All you need is an eye dropper, water, some sandy soil from the garden and some methylated spirits. It is best if you have a go at this activity first to determine that the soil students will be using is, in fact, water repellent.

Place a small pile of soil (a dessert spoon) on a dish or lid. Place a drop of water from the eye dropper onto the soil surface. If the water does sit on the surface but takes more than 10 seconds to soak in, the soil is water repellent. Often, the water will form into a ball and roll down the slope.

Students can repeat this but use a drop of diluted methylated spirits. This is prepared by adding 5 millilitres of methylated spirts to 100 millilitres of water. Methylated spirits will dissolve some of the coating, allowing water to soak in. Detergent will have the same effect as methylated spirits. If it still takes more than 10 seconds to soak in, the soil is very water repellent.

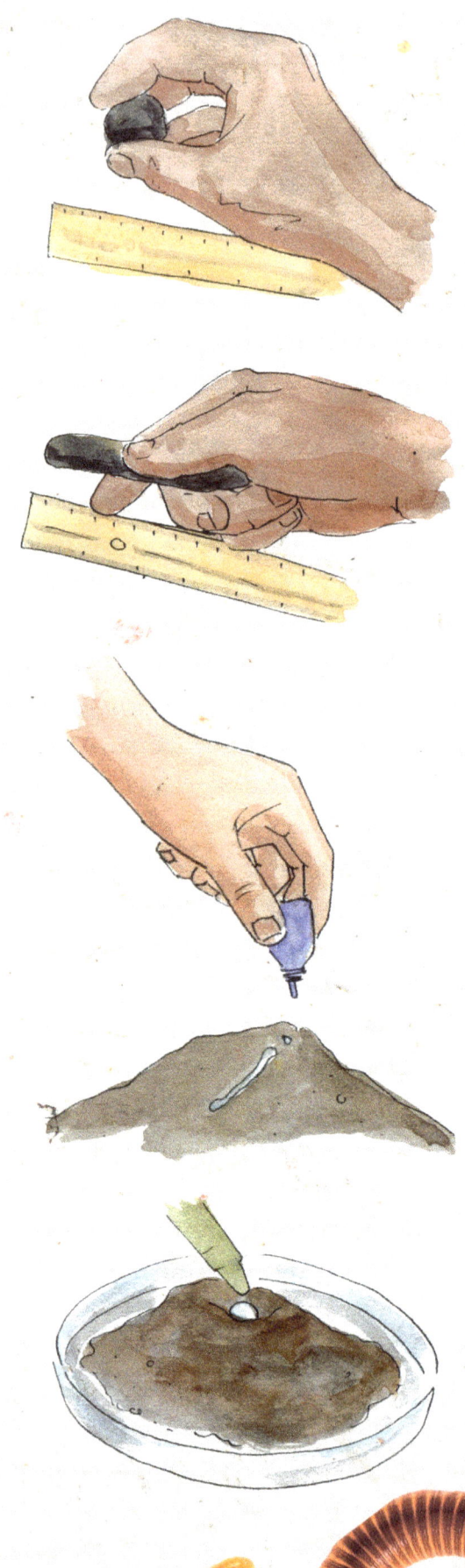

Teacher's Notes

EARTHWORMS

Gardeners and biologists love earthworms, almost as much as plants do! These burrowing creatures play a vital role in the ongoing health of the soil. As decomposers, they feed on the organic debris that they find on the soil surface. The dead plant and animal matter they digest contain nutrients, which are then released in their waste.

Worm faeces, or 'castings', are an ideal fertiliser. Micro-organisms break down the castings over time, slowly realising nutrients in the soil to be taken up by plants. Castings can be harvested from worm farms and added to potting mix or to the garden bed. Worm juice, a liquid by-product of worm farms, also serves a similar function.

PART 2

MAKE A SIMPLE WORM FARM

Worm farms like the one pictured here can be bought from hardware stores and gardening centres, but simple ones can also be made for classroom observation.

The easiest worms to acquire are manure worms. These are typically used in earthworm farms and require high levels of nutrients and water for them to survive and thrive. A one kilogram container of earthworms is more than enough to split into a dozen groups in the classroom.

To keep these worms satisfied, half fill a 2 litre ice-cream container with soaked peat or fine coir (coconut fibre). Add half a cup of aged or composted manure (not fresh, as it smells). Add manure worms and cover the container with a damp cloth (old clothes or paper towel). Don't put the container lid back on as this will restrict air supply and movement. A lidded container will also naturally heat up and 'cook' the worms.

Manure worms consume around their body weight each day, so weekly feeding is sufficient. Only a small amount of plant material or composted manure should be added when feeding. Add more food when the previous lot has mainly disappeared. Do not add food scraps.

Teacher's Notes

What do earthworms eat?

Earthworms love

- yard and garden waste
- food waste
- plant material
- a little soil or sand (important for their digestion process)
- wet paper and cardboard
- cow manure or sewage sludge

PART 2

Earthworms hate

- citrus
- onions
- garlic cloves
- spicy fruits and food products
- highly acidic foods
- poisonous plants
- metal and foil
- plastic
- chemicals
- oils
- solvents
- insecticides
- soaps
- paint

PROJECT

EARTHWORMS IN ACTION!

This activity allows students to see the effect that earthworms have on soil over time.

MATERIALS

- ✓ 2 litre plastic soft drink bottle or large jar
- ✓ white or yellow sand
- ✓ dark soil, with some organic matter
- ✓ water
- ✓ aged or composted animal manure – sheep, cow or horse
- ✓ earthworms – garden earthworms (generally introduced European earthworms) are ideal if you can find them. Otherwise manure worms (red wrigglers, tiger worms) can be used, provided they have lots of animal manure to eat

METHOD

1. Remove the top from the plastic bottle or large jar. Fill with alternate layers of sand and soil. The bottom two layers of dark soil should have some organic matter, such as animal manure, to provide food for the earthworms.

2. As you place each layer into the bottle, add some water – just enough to make the soil moist. This is important. Alternatively, you could just add moist soil to begin with but dry sand and soil flows better into the bottle.

3. Add several earthworms (gently) to the bottle – at least four. Make some holes in the lid, or place it loosely on top to allow air to flow into the bottle.

4. Place the bottle in a cool, dark place, checking every few days. Earthworms do not like sunlight or heat.

5. Students should eventually see the effect of the worms on the soil: moving, mixing, aerating and adding nutrients.

6. Once students have observed earthworms in action, carefully empty out the soil and earthworms into the garden.

Life in a Garden by Ross Mass | Reproducible

GARDENING SKILLS

COMPOSTING

Compost is an important ingredient for maintaining healthy soil, providing essential nutrients needed for plant growth. It's also quite easy to make – just follow the six M's of composting.

MATERIALS

For best results, a compost pile must be a mixture of plant and animal material. These provide the carbon and nitrogen that makes everything work properly. As a rule of thumb, add two shovelfuls of fresh animal manure to every wheelbarrow load of green plant material (e.g. weeds and lawn clippings). If you include some paper or dried leaves, add more animal manure. If you cannot access animal manure you can use blood and bone fertiliser or fish meal as your source of nitrogen.

MOISTURE

About 50 per cent of the pile should be water. If there is not enough water, then little decomposition occurs. Too much water will result in less air available in the heap, causing the pile to give off a smelly gas from the microbes that thrive in low-oxygen environments. To test for moisture, pick up some of your composting material. It should feel like a damp sponge. When you squeeze the material a few drops of water should drip out.

MIXING

Mixing helps add oxygen to the compost. The more oxygen present, the more heat is produced, promoting faster decomposition, less smell and fewer flies. Turn the pile as often as you can – once a week for the first three weeks and then leave alone. Turning with less frequency will also result in a good compost product, but will take longer. Be careful – turning compost too much can release valuable nutrients into the air and cause the pile to lose too much heat.

Continued...

GARDENING SKILLS

MICRO-ORGANISMS

When you start a new compost pile, you can add some 'aged' or cured compost from a previous effort to kick-start the new pile. This is not always necessary, as airborne bacteria quickly invade the pile and start reproducing.

MINERALS

Plants need minerals from the soil. You can add sand or small handfuls of rock or granite dust, loamy soil, crushed limestone and diatomaceous earth (a type of soft, crumbly rock). These all add nutrients to the pile, which are beneficial for growing plants.

MASS

There are two things to keep in mind here:

PARTICLE SIZE – the finer the organic material the faster the decomposition, so shredding is important. While it is best to shred the material you use in the compost pile, occasional bulky material such as wood chips and tree cuttings assist in aeration of the pile.

VOLUME – compost piles require a certain critical mass. If the pile is smaller than a cubic metre, it cannot maintain enough heat. Keep in mind that the pile shrinks as it decomposes. At the same time, making a compost pile too large can make turning and shifting the pile difficult, especially if students are to be involved in maintaining it.

SOME OTHER THINGS TO CONSIDER

You may be tempted to continually add material to your compost pile as you acquire it. But this will cause the pile to cool and the compost process to slow down, or even cease completely. It is best to collect organic material until there is enough for one big batch.

It is possible to have several compost batches going at once. It's worthwhile to build proper storage bays from wooden sleepers or concrete slabs. These can be easily covered with hessian, carpet or underfelt to reduce the smell and pests. While the end product may have a nice 'earthy' smell, the process of decomposition produces a range of noxious gases if the ratio of plant and animal materials, water and oxygen is not well balanced.

INVESTIGATION

BANANA BREAKDOWN

This simple experiment allows students to observe how decomposers break down organic matter and return nutrients to the soil. *It is set out here as a teacher demonstration, but can be easily adapted as a simple group activity.*

MATERIALS

- ☑ banana
- ☑ 1 sachet of yeast
- ☑ 1 teaspoon sugar (optional)
- ☑ 2–3 zip-lock bags

METHOD

1. Present a banana to the class and peel it. Ask students what will happen to the peel if it is left in the classroom. *It will go black, it will smell, it will start to rot.*

2. Ask students whether all things rot. *No, only objects that were part of living things.*

3. Show students the bag or sachet of yeast. Explain that yeast is a *decomposer*. It breaks down organic matter that can then be added to soil as compost.

4. Slice the banana in half and place each half in one of the two zip-lock bags. Add yeast to one of the bags and shake the bag to coat the banana. You may also wish to slice another banana and add a teaspoon each of yeast, sugar and warm water (no higher than 40 °C). Shake the bag to dissolve the sugar and to activate the yeast.

5. Over the course of 48 hours, students should return to the experiment and record their observations. Along with the rate of decomposition, students will also notice the bags with yeast swelling with air. This is caused by the respiration of the yeast.

Note: You may also undertake or repeat this activity using the banana skin. This also will change but will usually take a little longer than the fruit itself.

Banana half – no yeast

Banana half – sprinkled with yeast

Banana half – covered in yeast solution

TEACHER'S NOTES

MULCH

Every productive garden should have mulch covering the soil and around plants. Mulch protects the soil, reduces water loss and keeps the soil cool. Mulch also helps prevent the propagation of weeds, as weeds tend to prefer bare ground. Most mulches are made from shredded plant material but can also include other non-plant materials. When organic mulches break down, they provide nutrients for the soil and plants. These mulches are also the food eaten by slaters, mites and millipedes. These creatures are common in mulch piles but should be monitored to keep them from eating nearby plants. Some mulch can also be changed into compost.

ORGANIC MULCHES

Organic mulches are generally made from plant-based organisms. Animal manure can also be used as a mulch, but we think of manures more as fertiliser. Straw, hay, grass clippings, shredded plant materials (e.g. leaves, bark) and pine needles are the most common mulches used in gardens. Organic mulches eventually break down and become nutrients for plants.

INORGANIC MULCHES

These include natural materials such as stone, gravel and scoria (a volcanic rock), or man-made (synthetic) materials such as plastic sheeting (both clear and black), geotextile, vermiculite, hessian and cardboard. Rocks and stones are often used in dry landscapes as a mulch around trees as they are common in these areas.

LIVING MULCHES

Living mulches are low-lying plants that cover the ground. They spread over an area covering the soil and help minimise the risk of soil erosion. They are usually fast-growing, thick and hardy, enabling then to smother and out-compete weeds. It is important to manage the competitive relationship between the living mulch plant and the main crop. Creepers and groundcovers, such as sweet potato, make an ideal living mulch.

INVESTIGATION

PART 2

EVAPORATION

This simple experiment will allow younger students to observe the effect of evaporation, and how covering soil with mulch can prevent water from leaving the soil too quickly.

MATERIALS

- ☑ water
- ☑ jars with screw lid, or clear glass cup and aluminium foil
- ☑ textas
- ☑ rulers

METHOD

1. Explain to students that when water heats up, it becomes vapour. Have students recall times when they have seen water vapour (such as the steam from a kettle, or rising from hot food). When the ground is warm enough, water in the soil can become vapour and escapes from the ground. We may not see this happen, but on a hot day the soil can lose water very quickly.

2. Divide students into groups and have them use a measuring cup to fill two identical jars or clear plastic cups with the same volume of water so that it fills at least half the jar. Leave one jar uncovered, while covering the lid of the other with aluminium foil or the screw lid. Use a permanent marker to draw a line to mark the height of the water. Record the height of the water using a ruler and place the jars in a sunny spot.

3. Students should check on their jars at regular intervals throughout the day and record the height of the water using a ruler.

4. At the end of the day, students should make their final observation. If very little evaporation has occurred, carry this activity over to another day at least.

5. Ask students what they can conclude from their results. What can we do to stop water from evaporating from the garden? *Cover it.* Explain to students that we cover soil with mulch to stop water from leaving the soil too quickly.

ACTIVITY SHEET

EVAPORATION

PART 2

PREDICTION

Which jar do you think will lose the most water? _____

_____

_____

RESULTS

Measure the water level of your jars uisng a ruler a few times during the day. Each time you measure, write down the time and the water level in each jar.

JAR WITH LID

TIME	WATER LEVEL (MM)

JAR WITH NO LID

TIME	WATER LEVEL (MM)

CONCLUSION

Tick which jar had the least water at the end of the experiment: ☐ Jar with lid ☐ Jar with no lid

Why did one jar lose more water than the other? _____

_____

Life in a Garden by Ross Mass | Reproducible

INVESTIGATION

COMPARING MULCHES

This activity allows students to compare the effect of different types of mulch on soil temperature.

PART 2

MATERIALS

- ☑ different types of mulches, such as shredded plant material, gravel or stones, pine needles, straw and builder's plastic sheeting (black)
- ☑ thermometer (analogue or digital)

Notes: If you cannot find the space for this activity, try using 2 litre ice-cream containers half filled with sand, and placing a 30 millimetre layer of mulch on top. These containers can be kept in the classroom in a position where they can be heated by sunlight through a window.

If you can obtain a tensiometer or a soil moisture probe you can also measure changing levels of moisture.

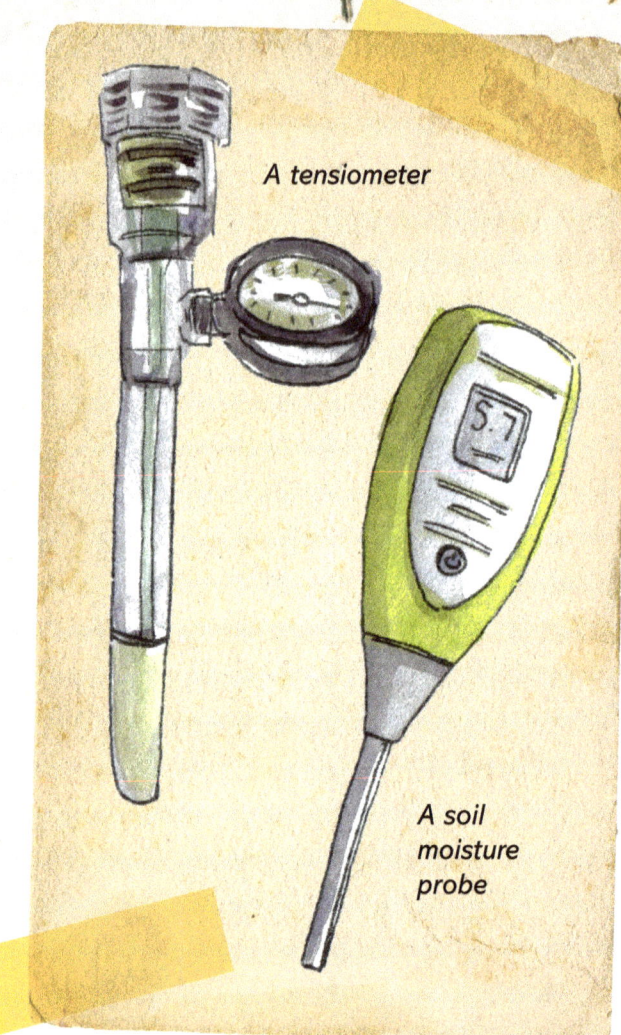

A tensiometer

A soil moisture probe

METHOD

1. Find an area that is usually in direct sunlight or an area that receives the same amount of sunlight each day. The soil must be even over the site – sand, cleared area, but not lawn. Place 50 millimetres of mulch over a 0.5 m² area. Space these mulch piles at least 1 metre apart. Keep one area as the control – no mulch at all. This will allow a comparison between all mulches and bare ground.

2. Over the next week, and at the same time each day, have students measure the temperature in the soil 2 centimetres below the centre of the mulch pile. Be careful if you are using an alcohol or mercury thermometer. You may have to gently dig away the soil, place and hold or support the thermometer and backfill. Let the temperature stabilise and take the reading.

3. Have students record these results using the provided worksheet, and discuss their findings. Readings of soil moisture add more complexity to this exercise. A digital soil moisture meter can be used for this purpose. A tensiometer is normally left at one site and measurements taken each day. A digital meter can be removed each day.

4. You should find that the temperature below any sort of mulch is a few degrees cooler than bare ground. You should also find some small differences between different mulches. Results may be difficult to interpret if the site is rained on or part of the site is in shade while other parts are in full sun. Similarly, soil moisture is normally greater under mulch piles than in bare ground.

ACTIVITY SHEET
COMPARING MULCHES

DIRECTIONS

Choose three mulches to test and compare them to the temperature of the soil with no mulch.

Describe the three mulches that you are going to test:

Mulch 1: Organic ☐ Inorganic ☐

Made from:_____

Mulch 2: Organic ☐ Inorganic ☐

Made from:_____

Mulch 3: Organic ☐ Inorganic ☐

Made from:_____

What time will you be testing your soil every day?_____

DATE	OUTSIDE TEMPERATURE	SOIL TEMPERATURE (NO MULCH)	SOIL 1 TEMPERATURE	SOIL 2 TEMPERATURE	SOIL 3 TEMPERATURE

PART 2

RESULTS

Make a line graph of your results here. Use a different colour for each soil sample (including the soil with no mulch). Add a scale for the temperature and day. Colour the appropriate boxes to make a key.

Temperature

Key:

☐ No Mulch

☐ Mulch 1:_____

☐ Mulch 2:_____

☐ Mulch 3:_____

Day

CONCLUSION

Which mulch kept the soil coolest? _____

Was there a mulch that showed the least change in temperature?_____

GARDENING SKILLS

TESTING SOIL MOISTURE AND WATERING PLANTS

In this activity, younger students will learn a simple technique for checking soil moisture. They will then use this method to determine whether or not their garden plants need to be watered.

PART 1: FINGER TEST

MATERIALS:

- ☑ flat tray containers, such as fast food containers or the bottom of an ice-cream container
- ☑ measuring cups – half and full cup (125 and 250 ml)
- ☑ dry soil – to nearly fill container

METHOD

1. Review the importance of water to both soil organisms and plants. Ask students how we can know whether a plant needs water. *The soil is dry, the plants look droopy, the leaves are turning brown.* Explain that they will be performing a simple test to determine if the soil is dry enough to require watering.

2. Provide each group with a container. Have students scoop some soil to fill the tray up to three-quarters full. (Any more than this and water runoff or spilt soil can occur.)

3. Ask students to place a finger into the soil to see what it feels like when dry. Get students to fill the half cup measure with water.

4. Have students carefully add the water as evenly as they can over the whole surface.

5. Once soaked in, get them to put their finger in to experience moist soil and to see how far the water has penetrated.

6. If the soil is still fairly dry, get them to add another measure of water to the soil. They may have to use the larger cup measure, depending on how much soil they have. Repeat the finger test.

7. Discuss observations with students, and mention that they can use the finger test to check whether their garden plants need water.

GARDENING SKILLS

PART 2: WATERING PLANTS

MATERIALS
- ☑ homemade watering cans (see setup)
- ☑ nursery watering can
- ☑ water source (outside tap)

SET-UP:

For this activity, homemade watering cans can be made from 2 litre plastic milk bottles. These do a better job of keeping younger students from spilling water on themselves, and can also provide a simple means for estimating how much water is being used on any one plant. Simply puncture six to 10 holes in the lid of the bottle using a kitchen skewer, compass or 2 millimetre drill bit. Water will not easily come out if the holes are too small, so make sure you test one before handing out to students.

Ideally, this lesson should be conducted when the plants have not been watered for a few days (perhaps on a Monday or after a long weekend) so that the soil will be reasonably dry. You may also choose to water a few areas of the garden beforehand so that students can recognise when a plant does not require watering.

METHOD

1. Review with students the things that plants need to live and grow. Remind them that plants need water almost every day, just like us. Ask, 'How do plants get water when people are not around?' *Rain*. 'What do we need to do when it hasn't rained?' *Water the plants*. Briefly explain that students will be testing the soil for dampness and, if necessary, they will be watering plants.

2. Take students outside, along with the watering cans. Students fill the bottle, screw on the lid and carry it out carefully to the garden area.

3. Spread students out so each person or group has one or two plants to water. Ask them to perform the finger test to determine if the soil is dry.

4. To water plants, students simply turn their watering can upside down, directing the nozzle towards the plant base. Squeezing the bottle will help increase the rate of discharge. Ensure that students know to water the soil and not the leaves. A small shrub of up to 1 metre will be able to take the whole 2 litres.

5. Have students also practise using a nursery watering can so they know how much water passes out through the nozzle. If they fill the nursery watering can with 2 litres of water, they can then compare the time taken using their homemade can and the nursery one.

6. If there are large trees to water, consider using a laundry bucket, which typically holds nine to 10 litres.

7. Have students feel the soil around the plant after watering to check if the plant needs any more water.

PART 3
FROM SEED TO PLANT AND BACK AGAIN

When children are intimately involved in the continued welfare of living things, they develop a greater appreciation for the natural world, and a lasting concern for environmental issues. Students not only gain an understanding of the natural processes at work but are able to make more meaningful connections between the food they eat and where it comes from.

The activities in this section follow the life cycle of a plant, from germination to seed production and dispersal. It also focuses on how human beings can be involved in the process, including planting, harvesting and preserving food.

TEACHER'S NOTES:

Seeds	42
Seed germination	51
Flowers and pollination	58

PROJECTS:

Mini hothouses	53
Terrariums	54
Butterfly feeder	60
Bee hotel	63
Products from herbs	71
Preserving food	77
Recipes for excess garden produce	80

GARDENING SKILLS:

Planting seeds	45
Harvesting vegetables and fruit	64
Collecting seeds	84
Seed bombs	85
Resprouting vegetables	86

INVESTIGATIONS:

What's inside a seed?	43
Germination in a jar	52
Stems and leaves	56
Fruit sorting	67

TEACHER'S NOTES

SEEDS

Almost all plants begin their lives as seeds. Seeds vary widely in size, shape and even texture, but most contain the following structures:

EMBRYO

The embryo is the structure that will one day become a new plant. The embryo usually consists of a radicle, which will develop into the root system, and the plumule, which will become the shoot of the new plant. Small leaves are sometimes visible on the plumule, depending on the type of seed.

ENDOSPERM

The endosperm provides the embryo with the nutrients it needs to begin to grow. The endosperm can be packed around the embryo or can be stored in structures called cotyledons. Most seeds can be classified as either monocots, having one cotyledon (such as wheat and corn), or dicots, containing two (like peas and beans). The carbohydrates, fats and proteins contained in the endosperm are a rich food source for humans and animals.

SEED COAT

Seeds are usually encased in a hard, protective outer layer called a seed coat. When the conditions are right, the seed coat will soften, allowing water and air to enter the seed and begin the process of germination. Often, the seed coat will weaken when exposed to water, but sometimes other elements, such as the heat of a fire, are needed.

INVESTIGATION

What's Inside a Seed?

In this simple activity, younger students will have the chance to open up a seed and identify its parts.

Materials

- ✓ large dried beans, such as lima beans, broad beans, lablab beans, butter beans, kidney beans
- ✓ soaked beans (see setup below)
- ✓ magnifying glass
- ✓ paper towels or paper plates, one for each student
- ✓ activity sheet: What's inside a seed?

Set-up

Soak some seeds for 4 to 6 hours to soften the seed coat. Tinned four-bean mix has butter beans and kidney beans, already softened so they are easy to cut open and push off the seed coat with your fingers. Alternatively, you may wish to begin this lesson at the end of the day and soak the dried beans overnight, rather than using two sets of beans (soaked and unsoaked).

Method

1. Distribute a dry bean seed to each student. Ask, 'What do you think this is?' *Bean or seed*. Explain that a bean is a type of seed. Ask, 'Where do you think it came from? How do you think a seed becomes a plant?'

2. Tell students that they will be opening up a seed to take a closer look inside. Invite them to try to open their seeds with their hands. They will likely be unable, or at least find it difficult.

3. Explain that this seed is not yet ready to grow. It has a special coat covering it. When it is ready to grow, a seed's coat will soften and will eventually be removed. Remind students that a plant needs water, soil, light and air to grow. Most seed coats will soften after being exposed to water.

4. Distribute soaked beans (or the larger ones from a four-bean mix tin). Students should place all seeds on paper towels to absorb excess water. How do they look and feel compared to the dried ones? Demonstrate how to gently peel away the seed coat with their fingernail. It should be much easier now. They may note that the seed has swollen. This is a precursor for germination.

5. Have students open their beans to see what is inside. Discuss what they find (see the teacher's notes on page 42). They can use a hand lens or a magnifying glass for a closer look.

6. Have students draw and label the inside of the seed using the activity sheet, What's inside a seed?

ACTIVITY SHEET
WHAT'S INSIDE A SEED?

Cut out the seed template below and fold it down the middle. On the inside, draw and label what you found when you opened up your seed. On the outside, write some definitions of the parts of a seed that you labelled.

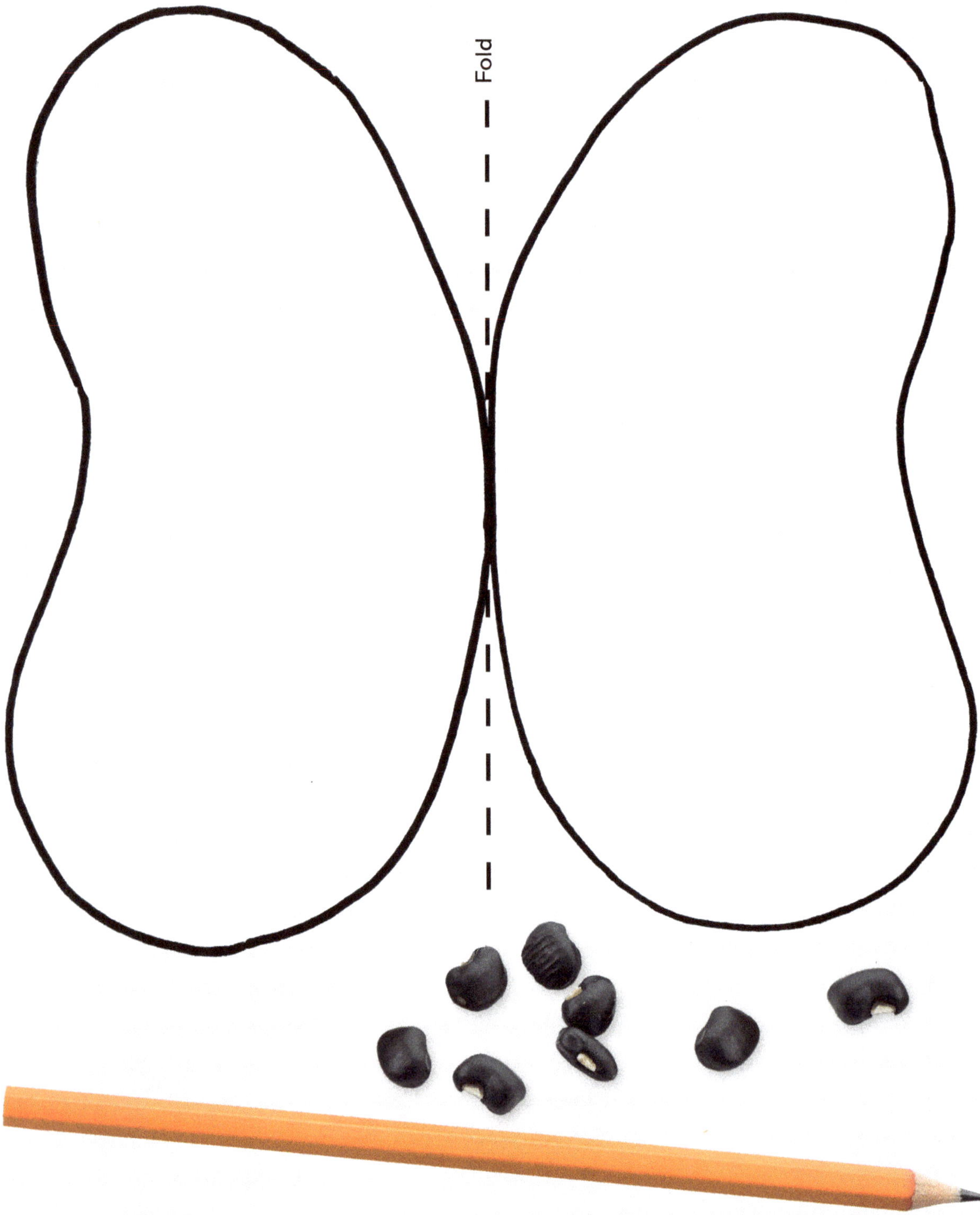

PART 3

Fold

Life in a Garden by Ross Mass | Reproducible

44

GARDENING SKILLS

PLANTING SEEDS

GROWING SEASONS

In schools it is often best to have two growing seasons. Plant winter crops in late March or early April. Plant the summer crops at the beginning of third term, so these can be harvested before the end of the school year. You may find some winter crops still maturing and fruiting well into the third term, so plan for some overlap. Some vegetables may not be ready for harvest by mid-December, so arrangements may need to be made for parents, teachers or gardeners to pick these and remove plant material during the summer break. You can find a growing guide for winter and summer vegetables on page 118, and information about building garden beds on page 6.

COMPANION PLANTING

Companion planting is a method of grouping plants together for their mutual benefit. Planting herbs with vegetables can help mask the shape, colour and smell of the vegetables, which confuses pests. The planting guide on page 117 contains some suggestions for plants that grow well together. Try not to grow the vegetables in a row or all together. Spread each vegetable type throughout the garden bed, and interplant these with other flowers, herbs and ground covers.

PREPARING THE GARDEN PLOT

Before any planting can occur the garden bed area may need attention. Old vegetable plants can be removed and a layer of new soil added to top up the bed. Add a layer of compost to make nutrients available to the new plants. Placing a 50 mm layer of coarse mulch over the bed helps keep the soil cool and minimise evaporation.

PART 3

Continued...

GARDENING SKILLS

PLANTING SEEDS

Many vegetable seeds can be planted straight from a packet. However, some seeds may require pre-treatment. Typically, this involves soaking the seeds for a few hours or even overnight. Find out about the seeds you are getting students to plant by reading instructions on seed packets, searching the web for seed treatment or asking your local nursery how best to grow them. Most seeds respond well to a soak in a jar of water, even for an hour or so. The influx of water triggers the germination process.

METHOD

Make a shallow furrow no more than 1 centimetre deep. Seeds are usually buried to a depth the same as their size to twice their size, so large seeds are buried deeper than small seeds. Large seeds can be individually placed about 5 to 10 centimetres apart, depending on how large the plant will grow, while small seeds are often sprinkled evenly along the furrow. Finally, gently cover the seeds with soil, and this may mean simply to push the furrow sides back together again. Make sure students do not bury the seeds too deeply. Use a garden hose or watering can to wet the soil.

PLANTING POTTED VEGETABLES AND HERBS

While seeds are an easy and cheap way to establish a garden, it is sometimes better to add seedlings and established plants to get the garden underway. Seeds may take several weeks to germinate and many months to grow to maturity. Buying seedlings, or raising your own plants beforehand as you get the garden areas ready, saves time and makes for an instant garden.

Continued...

GARDENING SKILLS

METHOD

Push any mulch to one side, and use your hands or a trowel to dig a hole the same depth as the seedling or pot. Carefully prise seedlings out of punnets by either pushing in the bottom of the punnet or using an icecream stick or teaspoon to lift the seedling up and out. The pots of larger plants may need to be squeezed to free the roots from the sides of the pot container. Place one hand, palm down, across the top of the pot so that the plant stem is between a person's thumb or first finger (or between first and second finger). Turn the hand and pot over and gently tap the bottom of the pot. The plant should slide out of the pot and the person's hand is holding the plant and soil together. Once a plant has been removed from its punnet or pot it should be planted straight away. Plant the seedling or plant, and firmly press the soil around the plant, being careful not to damage any roots. Carefully replace or scrape the mulch back around the plant, but keep it away from the stem. Plant roots will start to die if exposed too long to bright sunlight or hot conditions. If students remove all seedlings and these can't be planted quickly, have them place the seedlings or plants in a bucket of water. This is a helpful strategy to enable the plant to absorb water and help it overcome stress when planting.

ACTIVITY SHEET
PLANTING DIARY

Use the planting diaries to help students keep track of one or more garden plants. For example, drawing a picture of the plant's location may take the form of a simple drawing or a bird's eye view of the garden or garden bed. To measure the height of a plant, simply use a ruler or measuring tape positioned at the base of the plant. For older students, growth rate can be charted as a line or column graph. The diary can also be used to record observations from other activities in this book. The template on page 49 can be used as an in-depth case study of one plant and might be used by older students. A larger template on page 138 enables a broader snapshot of many plants.

PLANTING DIARY

PLANT NAME

PLANTED BY

ON

Go to page 138 for the diary template

DATE: HEIGHT:........CENTIMETRES

DATE: HEIGHT:........CENTIMETRES

DATE: HEIGHT:........CENTIMETRES

DATE: HEIGHT:........CENTIMETRES

DATE: HEIGHT:........CENTIMETRES

DATE: HEIGHT:........CENTIMETRES

ACTIVITY SHEET
PLANTING DIARY

DIRECTIONS

Fill in the information below and check your plant regularly (around once a week). Include the date, your observations of the plant and any other relevant information (for example, whether you watered the plant, or had to deal with problems like pests attacking your plant). You may also wish to take photos or draw pictures of parts of your plant (for example, any flowers it grows, or any damage done by pests).

PLANT NAME: _____ SEED ☐ OR SEEDLING ☐

DATE PLANTED: _____ **TYPE OF MULCH USED:** _____

Draw your plant's location in the garden bed and label any nearby plants.

GROWTH RATE

Create a line graph to track your plant's growth over time

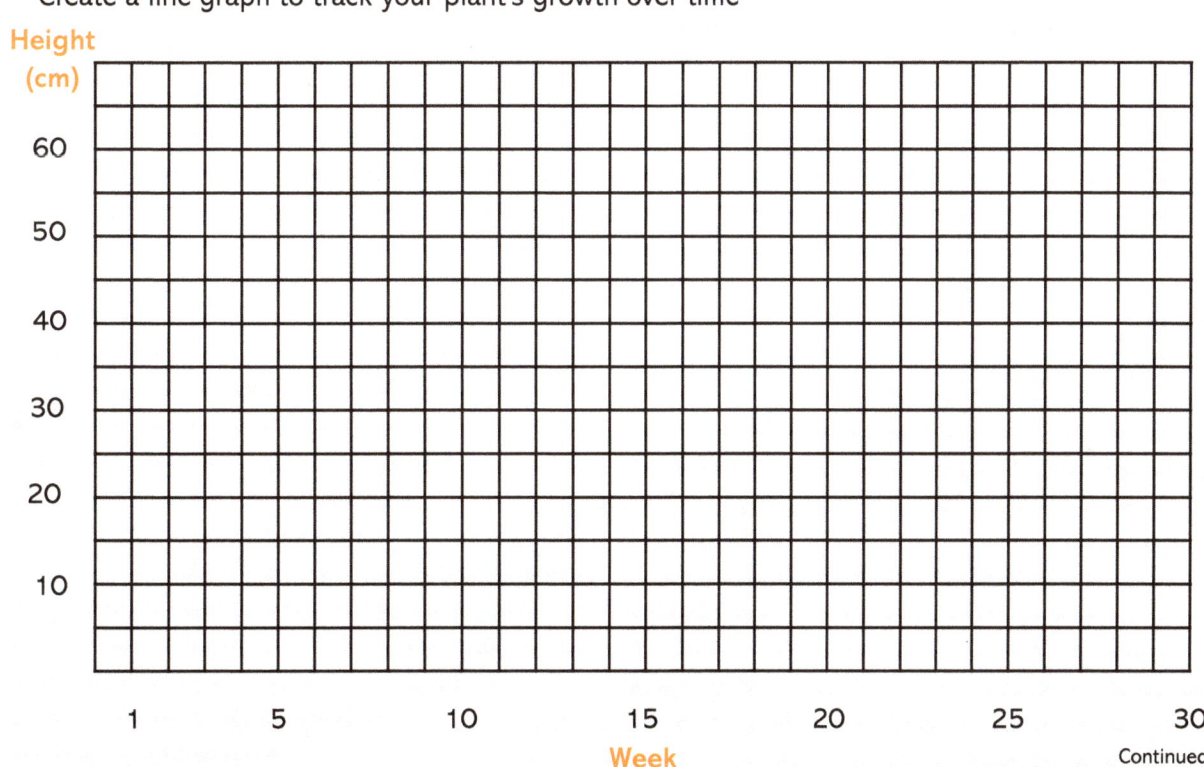

PART 3

Continued...

Life in a Garden by Ross Mass | Reproducible

ACTIVITY SHEET

PLANTING DIARY

DATE	OBSERVATIONS	PICTURE

PART 3

Teacher's Notes

Seed Germination

Germination is the process by which seeds sprout and start to grow into new plants. To germinate, a seed absorbs moisture from the soil, activating substances that release the nutrients surrounding the embryo. Soon afterwards, a shoot and root system begins to develop. The roots grow downward and the shoots upward, eventually breaking the soil surface and into the light. The plant leaves then form, which allows the plant to make its own food through photosynthesis. Plants also use the nutrients in the soil to grow and mature.

Every plant has a particular germination rate. This is usually expressed as a percentage and indicates the number of seeds out of one hundred that germinate. Some seeds have low germination rates (less than 40 per cent) while others can be close to 100 per cent.

Germination Requirements

Seeds only germinate under suitable conditions, requiring various levels of warmth, moisture and light. Most seeds germinate in spring, though some prefer colder weather. When the seed coat softens or is worn away, enough oxygen and water from the soil can enter to start the germination process. Too much water, however, deprives the soil of oxygen, causing the death of the seed.

Some seeds may require more specific conditions to trigger germination. Quandong seeds germinate after they pass through the digestive system of an emu or another bird. The acid in the bird's stomach weakens the seed coat, enabling water and oxygen to enter. Some native seeds need the heat and smoke from a fire to trigger germination. The heat and chemicals found in the smoke break the seed coat and allow the seeds to germinate.

PART 3

INVESTIGATION

GERMINATION IN A JAR

In this activity, students will be able to observe seeds as they germinate and sprout into new plants.

MATERIALS
- ☑ paper towel
- ☑ water
- ☑ large seeds (such as sunflower, pea and bean)
- ☑ large (wide mouth) jar, screw or push-in lid

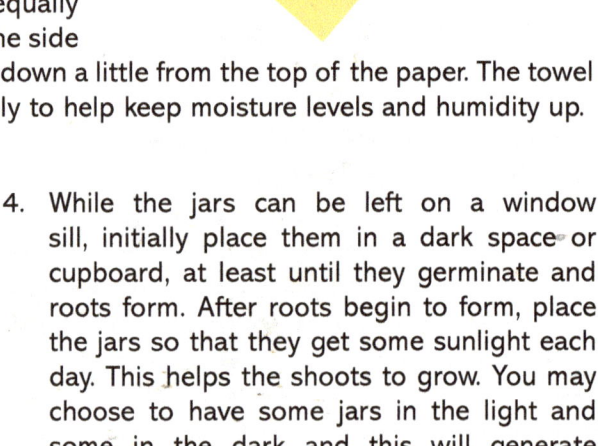

METHOD

Germination will occur faster if you pre-treat the seeds, such as soaking in water for a few hours or overnight.

1. Roll 3 or 4 sheets of paper towel into a cylinder and scrunch them enough to fit into the jar.

2. Carefully add water – enough to dampen the towel and to make a reservoir of about 2 centimetres at the bottom.

3. Gently add four seeds to the jar. Space them equally apart and place them into the towel, against the side of the jar so that they can be seen and maybe down a little from the top of the paper. The towel needs to support them. Place the lid on loosely to help keep moisture levels and humidity up.

PART 3

4. While the jars can be left on a window sill, initially place them in a dark space or cupboard, at least until they germinate and roots form. After roots begin to form, place the jars so that they get some sunlight each day. This helps the shoots to grow. You may choose to have some jars in the light and some in the dark and this will generate discussion with students.

5. Most seeds will take a couple of weeks before anything happens, but you might find some action after a week. Continue to monitor them until they can be planted in the garden. Be careful to remove them from the jar – including the paper. Young seedlings are easily damaged so consider planting the seedling along with any paper towel that it has attached to. The paper will eventually break down in the soil.

6. Students can record their observations in their books, or by using the planting diary on page 138.

PROJECT
MINI HOTHOUSES

Hothouses (also known as greenhouses or glasshouses) are used to create a warm microclimate to enable plants to survive, especially before reaching maturity. They use plastic or glass to shelter plants, trap heat and reduce moisture loss, and are often used to propagate plants in colder months or to keep cold-sensitive plants warmer.

MATERIALS

- ☑ soft drink bottle
- ☑ small seedling planted in garden or in a plant pot
- ☑ scissors or serrated knife

METHOD

1. Examine the drawings of different ways in which soft drink tops and bottoms can be used to cover the whole pot plant, just the plant in a pot or a seedling in the garden. Have students create the one/s as required by using scissors or a serrated knife to cut the top and base away. The bottle cap can be left on but often it is removed or at least loosened so that excess heat and moisture can escape. Too much moisture may encourage fungal disease.

2. Students should periodically inspect their plants to see how well they are growing, noting any moisture condensing on the bottle.

VARIATION: MINI HOTHOUSE USING TWO SOFT DRINK BOTTLES

Cut two soft drink bottles in half (you will only use three of the four pieces). One top section with the cap is used as a plant pot and one set of pieces are used to cover this, as shown here. You will need to punch or drill a few holes in the pot section or unscrew the cap enough so excess water can drain out.

PROJECT

TERRARIUMS

Terrariums are mini-gardens planted in a jar, bottle or large bowl. The various plants are often content living in their own mini-biosphere. Soon, cycles of nutrients, air and water are established to some degree, but some care is required to ensure plants are not subject to extremes of temperature, lack of oxygen or very high humidity. With some well-chosen plants and a few props, students can create some beautiful living dioramas.

MATERIALS

- ☑ large jar and lid (1 kg coffee jar, mason jar or kilner jar)
- ☑ selection of small plants. Succulents are ideal as there are many suitable varieties.
- ☑ potting mix, water
- ☑ garden pebbles
- ☑ assorted figurines (animals, houses etc. Bulk figurines can be purchased cheaply from Kmart or online). Students may also want to bring their own from home.

METHOD

1. Show students some examples of terrariums. There are many creative ideas to be found online. Explain that students will be making their own version of a terrarium.

2. Students should add some potting mix to the jar and add a little water to make it moist. They can then plant into the soil as carefully as they can, scraping away some of the soil to enable roots to be covered.

3. Set up the terrariums close to windows, but not in direct sunlight as this may overheat the jars and plants. Every week or two rotate the terrarium a little, so that each side will have access to sunlight and the plants will not grow in particular directions. Open the jar for a few hours every few weeks, add water if it seems dry, remove diseased leaves and plants as required and open the lid for a while if too wet.

Continued...

PROJECT

VARIATION: THE PLASTIC BOTTLE TERRARIUM

Obtain a 2 litre soft drink bottle. Cut the base off about one-third up. Fill the base with moist soil and plants as described previously. Place the cut top section back over the base and use sticky tape or clear masking tape to re-join the bottle and seal. The cap can be left on initially but may need removal or loosening if too much moisture builds up. Add additional water through the lid opening as required. Unscrew the cap occasionally to enable fresh air to enter.

INVESTIGATION

STEMS AND LEAVES

In this experiment, students will learn how water and nutrients are transported from the soil to the leaves of the plant for energy production. Part 1 of this experiment is an optional demonstration that will help older students understand capillary action, the process by which plants take up water.

MATERIALS

PART 1 (OPTIONAL)

- ☑ three drinking glasses or glass jars of the same size
- ☑ water
- ☑ food colouring of two different colours (blue and yellow work best)
- ☑ paper towel, or pieces of filter paper, folded into long strips

PART 2

- ☑ several glass jars or tall glasses
- ☑ food colouring of various colours
- ☑ flower cuttings of white flowers, such as carnations, roses or daisies
- ☑ sticks of celery with leaves still attached
- ☑ ice cream sticks or spoons
- ☑ sharp knife

Note: Since a change in colour begins to take place within a few hours, it is best to begin Part 2 in the morning so as to allow students to track the gradual change over the course of the day. Alternatively, set this up at the end of the day and inspect first thing the next morning.

METHOD PART 1: WATER IS STICKY!

1. Ask students what materials they think of when they think of something sticky. Suggest that water is a sticky substance and ask students in what ways this might be true.

2. Explain to students that water is sticky in two ways. Firstly, it sticks to surfaces like skin and hair (adhesion), which is why you need a towel to remove the water after a shower. Water molecules also like to stick together like links in a chain (cohesion). When one molecule moves, others will follow.

3. To demonstrate this, place three glasses side by side. Fill the left and right glasses with water. Add blue food colouring to the water in one glass and yellow food colouring to the other. Place half of one towel into the blue water and fold it over the rim of the empty cup in the middle. Do the same with the yellow cup. You will immediately see the water begin to climb up the paper towels and over into the middle cup (where the water will turn green). This gravity-defying process is called capillary action. Ask students to suggest reasons for why this occurs, knowing what they know about adhesion and cohesion. Ask students how this process might apply to plants before moving on to part 2.

Continued...

INVESTIGATION

METHOD PART 2: COLOURFUL PLANTS

1. Ask students what they do when they need water. *Turn on a tap.* How does the water get into the tap? *It is carried there by pipes.* Explain that a plant stem contains structures called xylem, which act like pipes that draw water from the roots to other parts of the plant. Tell students that they are going to see this in action through an experiment.

2. Place students into groups. Distribute one jar or glass to each group and have them fill the jar about one-quarter full with water.

3. Have students decide on a colour for their water. When they have decided, add a couple of drops of food colouring to the water. Younger students may be able to do this for themselves, perhaps while wearing gloves and art smocks to prevent stains. Use an ice-cream stick or spoon to stir and thoroughly mix the coloured solution.

4. Give each group a stick of celery and a flower to place in their jar.

5. Over the course of the day or the following morning, have students observe their plants and describe what is happening.

6. Discuss the results of the experiment. Using the knife, cut a section of the stem along its width to show students the colourful xylem (older students may do this themselves).

PART 3

Flowers and Pollination

Flowers are responsible for initiating a plant's reproduction cycle. Each flower contains structures that allow it to produce seeds to grow the next generation of plants.

Some plants are self-pollinating, while others must transfer pollen from one plant to another. Grasses, sedges and many deciduous trees rely on wind to carry their pollen. The pollen grains are usually light, and the flower parts are arranged so that pollen is exposed to passing wind. As you can imagine, most of the pollen that is produced and transferred by wind never reaches its destination.

Other plants rely on animals to transport pollen. Animals that perform pollination for the plant are called **pollinators.** While wind pollinated flowers are usually small and inconspicuous, animal-pollinated flowers are typically colourful, fragrant or full of nectar to attract insects, birds or mammals. Birds, bats, butterflies, wasps, bees and other insects pick up pollen on their bodies while harvesting pollen or drinking nectar from the flower.

Many flowers have developed ways to attract particular animals. For example, flowers that rely on night creatures, such as moths and bats, typically have white petals and a strong scent, while plants that rely on birds tend to produce nectar and have red flowers. This ensures that insects and other animals have a higher chance of visiting the same species of flower.

The seeds that are produced after pollination grow inside the flower and eventually can become new plants themselves. As a seed develops, the plant stores carbohydrates (starches and sugars), fats and proteins in it. This serves as nutrition for the plant until it can make its own food from the leaves that form.

Continued...

Teacher's Notes

Bees and Pollination

Bees collect pollen from flowers which they use as food. Their legs are specially adapted to enable them to harvest and transport pollen to their hive.

When bees become covered in pollen, they use a notch in their front leg to wipe and clean their antennae. They use their front legs to transfer the pollen from the flower to their rear legs which have a pollen sac to store pollen.

Australia has about 1500 different native bee species, which are spread throughout all states and all climate zones. One group, the stingless bees, are only found across the top of Australia, while others, such as species of the leaf-cutter bee group and the resin bee group, are found in every state. Species of all of the 10 groups of native bees are found in Queensland, but species of only five groups are found in Tasmania.

The majority of native bees are solitary insects, unlike the social bees we often associate with honey production and bees in our gardens. Solitary bees utilise hollows and crevices in structures and soil to lay their eggs or store small amounts of nectar, which is used as food as the young develop. Solitary bees do not make honey, while native social bees do.

PROJECT
MAKE A BUTTERFLY FEEDER

Butterfly feeders are a great way to attract some beautiful insects to pollinate your garden plants! They need watery solutions to obtain the nourishment they need.

Butterflies respond to different colours and need a variety of different feeding platforms to accommodate their proboscis, which varies in length among species. Besides sugar solutions, butterflies respond to amino acids, salt and a variety of fruit.

Here are two different feeders to try, but you can find many other versions online. Students can experiment with different colours or solutions and observe which feeder seems to attract the most butterflies.

FLOWER FEEDER

MATERIALS

- ☑ wooden dowel or skewer
- ☑ tape
- ☑ flower template (provided)
- ☑ bottle cap
- ☑ cotton balls
- ☑ sugar
- ☑ water
- ☑ PVA glue
- ☑ pipette

METHOD

1. Have students decorate and cut out their flower template and attach it to the dowel or skewer with tape. You may wish to encourage students to find out what colours or patterns will be most successful in attracting butterflies.

2. Attach the bottle cap in the centre of the flower using PVA glue. Add a small amount of glue to the inside of the bottle cap and attach a cotton ball to it.

3. Create a sugar and water solution (1 part sugar to 10 parts water), and use a pipette to soak the cotton ball in the solution. The sugar solution provides butterflies with nourishment and energy.

4. The feeder is now ready for the garden. It is better to attach it somewhere off the ground to help prevent ants and other insects from discovering it before the butterflies do.

Continued...

PROJECT

PLATE FEEDER

Made by suspending an old saucer or a jar lid on string from a tree, this feeder can be decorated with bright flowers and fruit to attract the butterflies.

MATERIALS

- ☑ large jar lid or ceramic saucer
- ☑ string
- ☑ soft fruits – banana, strawberry, mango, watermelon
- ☑ drill and 3 mm bit
- ☑ option – sponge and sugar solution

METHOD

1. Have students either tie string to three holes equidistant on a plastic lid, or make a string basket to support a saucer.
2. Cut up small sections of fruit and supply two to three pieces to each student or group.
3. Go out into the garden area and get students to tie the string ends to a branch so that the lid is supported and hanging down. Place the dish in a semi-shaded position.
4. Arrange some fruit pieces on the dish and leave for a few hours. During breaks or at other times students can visit their plate and observe butterflies in action. The fruit may need replacing every second day, or as it starts to decay and smell.
5. Instead of fruit, students can place a 30 millimetre square section of coloured sponge and add some sugar solution to it. Try different coloured laundry sponges and see which ones (colour) attract butterflies. While you can use a dyed, synthetic kitchen sponge, a natural sea sponge (if you can obtain) is safer for butterflies and other insects to feed from.

PART 3

ACTIVITY SHEET
DESIGN A FLOWER!

DIRECTIONS

Colour and cut out the flower below. Add a bottle cap with your bait to the centre and attach it to a dowel or skewer with tape. Place it in the garden to attract some friendly butterflies!

PART 3

Life in a Garden by Ross Mass | Reproducible

PROJECT
MAKE A BEE HOTEL

In this class activity, students will be making a 'bee hotel' which is a collection of different sized tubes and holes in timber, which may be used by different species of native bees, and other insects. It is also important to have flowers and plants nearby to attract them, as nectar and pollen are the food sources for these types of insects. A list of plants for attracting beneficial insects is available on page 132. Some extra adult support is ideal for helping students construct their designs.

MATERIALS

- ☑ bamboo culms (stems) 20 cm long and various internal diameters 3 to 10 mm. Make sure one end is blocked (use the node as one end and cut the shaft to required length)
- ☑ pieces of timber 15 to 20 cm long, which may be used as packers and fillers
- ☑ hand or electric drill, with assorted drill bits 3 mm to 10 mm
- ☑ 100 mm PVC pipe or planks of timber (for roof, walls of box)
- ☑ option: pole or stake to mount the bee hotel off the ground

METHOD

1. Students can work in groups to design and make their bee hotel. Several interesting patterns can be made using different diameters of bamboo or pipe. Plenty of examples can be found online.

2. Start placing bamboo culms into the PVC pipe or sandwiched in-between the timber walls of a box. Keep forcing these so that the culms are held tightly in place. Use smaller pieces of timber as fillers to pack and hold the culms and fill 'dead space' as the hotel is built.

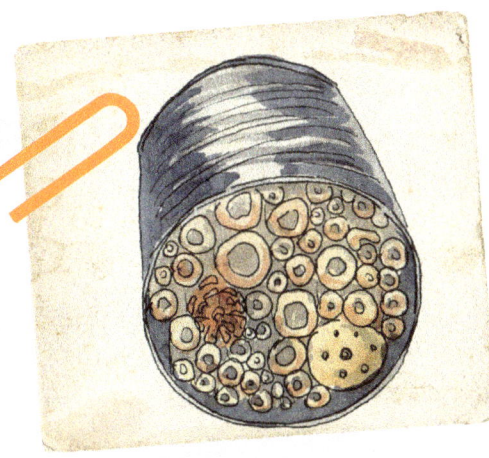

3. Use a drill and various drill bits to make holes in other timber pieces to give the bees alternative homes.

4. Place and secure other timber planks around the pipe to protect it from excess sunlight and rainfall. The hotel needs shelter.

5. Bee hotels should be mounted on a pole or placed on a wall that is somewhere from 1–2 metres high.

6. Periodically check whether your bee hotel has had any 'guests'. This may take some time, especially if you started this project in winter, so be patient.

GARDENING SKILLS

HARVESTING GARDEN VEGETABLES AND FRUIT

Because of the vast differences in climate, soil and other conditions, the time to harvest your produce varies from one location to another. Teachers should endeavour to find local information from organic garden or permaculture groups. Below you'll find some basic information on how to know when to harvest your garden plants and any techniques that will make picking a particular food easier.

ASPARAGUS
Harvest when the spears are 10 to 15 centimetres tall. Twist and break them off at ground level. New spears will grow in their place.

BEANS
Pick from the plant while pods are still very green, before you see seeds bulging.

BEETROOT
You can harvest and eat the leafy tops at any time. They are generally ready once you can see the root break the soil surface.

BROCCOLI
Once the head has a decent size, cut it off. Continue to grow the broccoli, since secondary (smaller) heads will grow and these can be plucked when you require. If you see flowers starting to emerge (as warmer weather approaches), it's too late. However, the flowers can be eaten too.

BRUSSEL SPROUTS
Harvest when the sprouts are about 3 to 4 centimetres long. Twist or cut off from the stem.

CABBAGE
Cabbage should be around 15 centimetres in diameter. Gently squeeze the cabbage head. If it feels firm, it is ready to be harvested.

CAPSICUM
Harvest these when the outside is reasonably large, firm and starting to change colour (usually from green to red or yellow).

CARROTS
Carrots can be difficult to judge. One technique is to push away the soil to expose the top of the carrot. If this looks thick then you can assume it is a good length. But this is not always the case, so pull one to see. If this appears to be a fair size then you can harvest the rest of the crop. Carrots can stay In the ground for a while, so harvest as you need. Remember though, the longer you leave them, the woodier they become.

CAULIFLOWER
Harvest when the head of the cauliflower is completely white and the surface of the head is relatively smooth.

CORN
The top ear (cob) is always the first to ripen. When the corn tassels dry and turn dark brown all the way to the husk, the corn is ripe.

Continued...

GARDENING SKILLS

CUCUMBER
Cucumbers take about 50 to 70 days to ripen, at which point they should be a dark green colour, and feel smooth and firm.

EGGPLANT
The fruits should be reasonably large, firm and shiny. They are difficult to tear off, so cut them from the stem instead.

GARLIC
Garlic has a long growing season – up to eight months. The bulbs are ready when their tops (green leaves) start to wilt and turn brown. Dig them up and brush off the dirt, rather than washing.

KALE
Kale leaves can be harvested over the growing season as others will grow back to take their place. The leaves should have a firm, sturdy texture.

LEEKS
Harvest leeks when they are about 2 to 3 centimetres in diameter.

LETTUCE (HEAD)
Harvest when the head feels full and firm when squeezed gently.

LETTUCE (LEAF)
Harvest the outer leaves once the plant is well established. Allow the younger, inner leaves to grow.

ONIONS AND SHALLOTS
Onions and shallots can be dug up once their foliage begins to wilt.

PARSNIPS
Once the leaves have died, you can pull from the ground.

PEAS
Feel the pods to check the size of the peas, then shell some to check. The peas should be smooth and firm.

POTATOES
Potatoes take at least four months to grow. Carefully pull back the soil to expose a few tubers. Harvest if they are the size of a hen's egg.

SQUASH
Harvest as soon as they reach a desirable size. The stem tends to die off as a sign that they are ripening.

TOMATOES
Tomatoes are picked when their colour turns deep orange to red. Large ones can be picked while green and then placed in a brown paper bag to self-ripen.

TURNIPS
Turnips can be harvested from the time they are the size of a golf ball and larger. Smaller roots are especially tender. Don't let the roots grow larger than a tennis ball or they'll become tough.

ZUCCHINI
Harvest when they reach at least 10 centimetres long, but don't allow them to grow too large, as they will not be as tender and will produce larger seeds.

Continued...

GARDENING SKILLS

TREE FRUITS

APPLES AND PEARS
Hold and twist apples and pears. If they easily come away they are ripe.

PEACHES, PLUMS AND NECTARINES
Ready when they become slightly softer to touch.

BERRIES AND CURRANTS
These should be evenly coloured. Leave blackcurrants and blueberries for up to a week after they seem to have their darkest colour.

The following table is a general guide for harvesting fruits, and may not be applicable to your area. The harvesting of many fruits may be spread over several months. For example, varieties of apples may mature from November to May, with most ripening February to April.

MONTH	WHAT FRUITS CAN BE HARVESTED
JANUARY	PEACHES, NECTARINES, PLUMS, APRICOTS
FEBRUARY	GRAPES, APPLES, WATERMELON, ROCKMELON, PEARS
MARCH	PRUNES, QUINCE
APRIL	PERSIMMON
MAY	FEIJOA
JUNE	LEMONS
JULY	KIWI FRUIT, MANDARINS
AUGUST	ORANGES, GRAPEFRUIT
SEPTEMBER	BANANAS
OCTOBER	STRAWBERRIES
NOVEMBER	CHERRIES
DECEMBER	MANGOES, AVOCADOS, BANANAS, BLUEBERRIES, TOMATOES

INVESTIGATION

FRUIT SORTING

In this activity students will examine a number of fruits and create a set of cards to identify and classify different types of fruits.

Fruits are foods that contain seeds. The fruit is most often the swollen ovary of a flower, with its seeds found inside. Some fruits have other parts of the flower that develop to become the part we eat. The structure of fruit can vary considerably, so the character and position of seeds tends to be the most common way to classify them, as shown in the diagram below:

FRUITS

DRY

SPLITTING
PEAS
BEANS

NON-SPLITTING
ALMONDS
HAZELNUTS

SUCCULENT (FLESHY)

BERRY (SEEDS IN FLESH)
TOMATO
CUCUMBER
BANANA

DRUPE (SINGLE SEED)
PLUM
APRICOT
PEACH

POME (OVARY IS CORE)
APPLE
PEAR

Continued...

INVESTIGATION

SET-UP

For younger students, it is better to pre-cut the fruit immediately before this lesson. Be aware of any allergies that your students may have. You may wish to provide gloves or a tub of soapy water to mitigate mess.

MATERIALS

- ☑ a variety of fruits (ideally you should include some unfamiliar fruits, or ones that are often confused with vegetables, such as tomatoes or cucumbers)
- ☑ plastic knives or dinner knives (optional for younger students)
- ☑ paper plates
- ☑ rubber gloves for students (optional)
- ☑ activity sheet: fruit flash cards

PART 3

METHOD

1. Brainstorm with students the characteristics of a fruit. Guide students to understand that a fruit is the part of the plant that contains seeds.
2. Explain to students that they are going to cut up some fruit to see where the seeds are located and what they look like.
3. Give each student a piece of fruit and have them slice their fruit in half (lengthways for bananas) and identify the seeds and other aspects such as the colour and texture of the flesh.
4. Students can then move around the room and observe the other fruits their classmates have been given.
5. After washing and drying their hands, students will fill out the handout and create cards with sketches of the fruit and its seeds.
6. Explain to students that scientists often sort living things into groups based on what they have in common. This is called classification. Give students time to sort their cards into groups based on the common features they see. Do not give them a category to sort them into. Ask students to share how they have sorted their fruit and why. Discuss which categories seem to make the most sense, before explaining how fruit is generally classified (see the diagram in the background notes).

EXTENSION

Play a fruit matching game with pairs of students. One student will lay out cards with the fruits face up, while the other will place their seeds face up. Each student can then take turns attempting to match the seeds with the correct fruit.

ACTIVITY SHEET

FRUIT FLASH CARDS

DIRECTIONS

Draw the fruit you have seen in the boxes on the left. Write the name of each fruit on the line. In the box on the right, draw what its seeds look like. Cut along the dotted lines and then fold along the solid line. Glue together so that the fruit and seeds appear on opposite sides of the card.

FRUIT | Fold | **SEED**

PART 3

Continued...

ACTIVITY SHEET

FRUIT | Fold | SEED

PART 3

Life in a Garden by Ross Mass | Reproducible

PROJECT
MAKING PRODUCTS FROM HERBS

Herbs are plants with properties that can be useful in cooking, medicine and relaxation. Below are a few simple ways you can put your garden herbs to use.

DRIED HERBS

Drying herbs is the first step in making herb pillows and potpourri. The main problem you may encounter is that herbs with high moisture content in their leaves (such as basil, mint, lemon balm and oregano) may become mouldy as they dry. Low moisture herbs, such as rosemary, marjoram, dill and thyme, dry well.

Pick branches of a particular herb and bundle four to six of these together in a bunch. Tie with string or an elastic band and peg to a line supported in a cupboard or dark place. Do not leave exposed to direct sunlight. The idea is to ensure the essential oils are kept within the plant material as it slowly dries. Never use an oven, dehydrator or food dryer to dry fresh herbs.

POTPOURRI

Potpourri is a mixture of dried fragrant herbs which are used to provide a natural scent to the surroundings. Often coloured petals and flowers are included to provide variation and a pleasing visual effect. The mixture is placed in a jar with a perforated lid, so the perfume can waft into the room.

PLANT PARTS	EXAMPLES OF HERBS OR PLANTS TO USE
Seed	Fennel, dill
Flowers	Lavender, rose, rosemary, jasmine, marjoram
Wood shavings	Cedar, juniper, pine
Leaves	Pelargoniums, lavender, mint, lemon balm
Peel	Lemon, orange
Fruit (dried)	Allspice (*Pimenta dioica*), cloves

For this activity combine a few of the dried herbs students have prepared. Get them to break these into small pieces with their hands or cut with scissors.

Add a few fresh leaves, petals or flowers to provide colour. Place the mixture into a wide-mouthed jar which has half-a-dozen holes drilled in the lid so the perfume can drift into the air.

HERB PILLOW SACHET

A number of fragrant herbs are stuffed into a small pouch and tied. The bag is placed inside a pillowcase, so when a person goes to bed the subtle scents relax them as they go to sleep.

Herbs to use include lavender, chamomile, rosemary, rose petals, mint and lemon verbena. If you have these available, try mugwort, catnip, sweet marjoram and hops. Once you have chosen your herbs, simply dice them and stuff into a sachet bag before tying it off with string. Sachet bags can easily be found online, or you can sew them yourself using square pieces of fabric 150 mm × 150 mm.

PROJECT

FOOD AND DRINK

BOUQUET GARNI

A bouquet garni is a bundle of herbs which are tied up with string or filled into a small sachet. They are used to add flavour to foods with a high liquid content, like soups and stews. It is usually removed prior to eating the meal. Various herbs can be used but the most common are some combination of thyme, bay leaf, basil, rosemary, parsley and sage. You can also include certain vegetables in the bouquet, such as celery, onion and leek.

METHOD

After choosing suitable herbs from the garden, use three or four herbs and one vegetable part. Students tie the bunch together with string. Place these in a large ziplock bag for students to take home.

HERB-INFUSED OIL

INGREDIENTS AND EQUIPMENT

- ☑ oil – one cup of olive, grapeseed, rice bran, coconut or almond oil
- ☑ dried herbs – three teaspoons of chamomile or calendula flowers, or the leaves of peppermint or lavender
- ☑ jar and lid
- ☑ cheesecloth or similar to act as filter
- ☑ for hot infusion: double steamer (boiler) or pot in a hot water bath

METHOD

Place herbs in the oil in a jar. There are two ways to undertake this. Cold infusion occurs when dried herbs are placed in an oil and left in a warm place, but not in direct sunlight, for a few weeks. The essential oils slowly are absorbed into the oil. Filter oil to remove herb fragments.

A hot infusion is made when the mixture of herbs in an oil is heated for about thirty minutes, usually in a water bath or a double boiler (which is a pot in another pot) so the oil is not overheated. The fragrances in the herbs are absorbed quicker. Allow to cool and filter herb pieces out of oil.

The herb-infused oil can be used in the lip balm recipe on page 74.

Continued...

PROJECT

SPEARMINT ICE BLOCKS

Any edible mint will suffice, such as common mint, spearmint and Moroccan tea mint. Do not use basil mint, eau de cologne or other mints with strong fragrances. Cut or tear a spearmint leaf into two or three pieces, and place one piece in every ice cube space in the tray. Fill with water and then freeze. When required, remove these from the tray and add to a glass of water (or simply suck on them).

HERBAL TEAS

Herbs used in tea are a great addition to any garden. Add two or three leaves or dried flowers to boiling water and allow it to infuse for a few minutes. Leave a little longer for a stronger flavour. If desired, add a little honey or a slice of lemon for a sweeter brew. Some herbs work well together as blends, including green tea and bergamot, and lemon verbena and cinnamon. Feel free to experiment, and have the class develop their own blends to take home.

Some common herbal teas include:

- ☑ English or Roman chamomile
- ☑ German chamomile
- ☑ lemon balm
- ☑ lemongrass
- ☑ lemon verbena
- ☑ peppermint
- ☑ spearmint

PART 3

PROJECT

SKIN CARE

HERBAL LIP BALM

INGREDIENTS AND EQUIPMENT

- ☑ 10 g beeswax (soy wax and cocoa butter can be used)
- ☑ 10 g shea butter*
- ☑ 10 g herb-infused oil (if you cannot source or make, then use olive oil and 6 drops of an essential oil such as lavender or peppermint)
- ☑ sweetener, such as stevia, hermesetas, xylitol or similar powder or liquid
- ☑ option: colour pigment, flavours. You can source these through online sales and various 'kits'. All are safe to eat
- ☑ double pot boiler or pot in hot water bath
- ☑ wooden spoon
- ☑ small wide-mouthed jars, with screw lids (baby food jars)

*The shea butter is not essential and it may be difficult to obtain but makes the balm creamier and easier to apply. You can substitute this with cocoa butter or coconut oil. The coconut oil melts with body heat.

METHOD

1. Set up double pot boiler. In the top pot add wax (shaved if possible) and shea butter.

2. Heat over hot water until wax and butter has melted and stir to mix thoroughly. You can heat gently the pot on the stove without a water bath, but ensure you do not overheat or burn the ingredients.

3. Allow to cool a little and then add infused oil and/or drops of essential oil. Stir to mix. Add one-quarter of sweetener, and any colour pigments, glitter or flavours. Before they place mixture in jars students can dip their finger in the mixture and taste. They might want to add more sweetener.

4. While still warm pour into smaller jars. The balm should set like a toothpaste. If too hard, heat up again and add a little more oil. Likewise if too runny, add wax. Be aware, too much wax and it tastes like wax, so this is not ideal.

5. The lip balm should last a year or more, but the longer you leave it the harder it tends to get.

There are many similar recipes so it is a matter of try and see.

Continued...

PART 3

PROJECT

This activity could easily be changed for students to make a healing balm. Substitute sweetener and herb-infused oil for a small amount of tea tree oil or calendula flowers or similar herbs that have therapeutic qualities. A healing balm is used to cover scratches and wounds on the skin, chafed lips and skin conditions like eczema.

EXTRACTING ESSENTIAL OILS

Steam distillation is used to extract oils from the leaves of many aromatic herbs and plants. This is how lavender and rosemary oil, tea tree oil and eucalyptus oil are produced. The activity below is designed to be a class demonstration. You will need a lot of leaf or flower material, so a couple of large overgrown rosemary or lavender bushes or similar scented plants are required. Use the flowers of lavender for oil but the leaves of most other scented plants.

Students can harvest the material from the plants or at least strip the leaves from the branches. An old pressure cooker is ideal but a steamer can be used as well. There is a lot of preparation (of material) needed for such a small amount of oil that is made. This itself is a discussion with students, and helps to explain the high cost of these oils. Lavender flowers could yield over 2 per cent oil by weight, but most herbs and scented plants have less than 2 per cent. This includes rosemary, tea tree and eucalypts. Other plants may only yield 1 per cent or less.

Most essential oils have boiling points 175 °C or higher, but steam distillation allows the components of these oils to vaporise, be condensed back into liquid and then easily separated from the water fraction.

The biggest challenge for this activity is finding or building the steamer. You should use a pressure cooker but a large pot with a pressure-tight lid (or at least one you can clamp down) can be modified. You can even use a kettle, with pipework from the nozzle, passing steam through a container of leaf or flower material and then onto the condenser. The important thing is to produce high temperature steam. This technique is not that efficient so, if nothing more, you can smell the hydrosol (the distillate which is a watery mixture) as evidence of oils and scents in the water.

MATERIALS

- ☑ pressure cooker. You need a large one – 5 litres or more. Older style cookers have a simple nozzle that a hose can slip onto. Modern cookers may not be suitable
- ☑ 2 m rubber hose (it needs to withstand heat)
- ☑ large bowl for water bath
- ☑ jar (to collect condensate)
- ☑ colander, steamer dish or similar that fits inside pressure cooker
- ☑ stove or camping gas burner
- ☑ wide-mouth jar or small saucepan (to remove hot water from the water bath)
- ☑ herb or other scented leaves – such as rosemary, tea tree, eucalyptus, lemon or pelargonium. If you have enough flowers, then try lavender.

Continued...

PROJECT

METHOD

1. Strip leaves from branches. Slide the twig from the top to the bottom between your thumb and forefinger. You can also slide from bottom to top and this technique is useful for many branched plants such as rosemary.

2. Place the colander inside the cooker. Add water to cover the base of the colander. The important thing here is that you want to use steam to rise through the leaf material and out of the cooker. Too much water generally results in boiling the leaves and oil vapour is lost.

3. Fill the colander as much as you can (yes, that is a lot of plant material).

4. Fix rubber hose to pressure release valve, wind in a coil and place this in a bowl of cold water. The end should be placed in the collection jar.

5. While heating and as steam is produced, endeavour to keep the coiled tubing under the water (maybe held down with a weight). If the water starts to heat up, scoop some of it from the bowl and replace this with more cold water.

6. This apparatus is crude and invariably condensate stays in the rubber tubing, so you will need to carefully lift the coil up and out of the bath and drain into the jar. It will be very hot so be careful!

7. You need to keep this going to obtain at least one to two cups of condensate or until you see oil floating on the water. The heating process may take half-an-hour to one hour. If too much steam is pouring out of the collecting jar, then the water bath is too hot. The removal and topping up with cold water may need to occur several times.

8. Turn off the heat, let it cool and pass the jar around to students to smell. You might find some oil has condensed above the water on the jar sides. Swirl the condensate around to wash this down. You don't need to separate the oil from the water but, if you freeze the condensate, the oil can be poured off.

PROJECT
PRESERVING FOOD

Garden produce can be preserved in a variety of ways. Drying drives off almost all moisture so that micro-organisms and mould cannot survive or breed. Bottling uses heat to kill micro-organisms, and then sealing in a partial vacuum as the solution cools down. Pickling immerses food in an acidic solution, such as vinegar, in order to create an inhospitable environment for moulds and bacteria.

DRYING

While you can buy commercial food dryers you can make a simple one by stretching some flyscreen across a wooden frame. Ideally, if air can circulate underneath as well, the fruit will dry more evenly.

There are a few different versions of solar dryers, but they rely on the heat of the sun to cause air to heat up and to move upwards and through the trays, slowly drying the fruit. Several trays, often with flywire mesh as the base, allow air to move through and over the thinly-sliced fruit and vegetables.

Solar dryers are typically used to dry fruit as a method of food preservation. Sliced fruit, meat and herbs generally take a day or two to dry. Not all of the moisture is lost, so fruit tends to be leathery and a little flexible.

Fruits that dry well include apples, pears, apricots, peaches, nectarines, bananas and lemons.

METHOD

1. Cut fruit into slices about 5 millimetres thick. Bananas can be cut lengthwise too, after peeling. The skins of most fruits can be left on. Remove the core and any large seeds.
2. Place fruit slices over the screen. Ensure that there is space between the slices.
3. Place in direct sunlight. If there is a possibility of insect attack you may need to cover with another layer of flyscreen, supported a little above the fruit.
4. Most fruits need at least a day or two to dry, so you may need to bring the trays inside at the end of the day, and place out again in the morning.
5. The fruit should be flexible and not burnt or crisp. Sample to decide if the fruit needs further drying.

Continued...

PROJECT

BOTTLING

Bottling is a technique for storing and preserving produce in jars and bottles.

Produce must first be properly prepared. For example, the seeds, peel and the core of fruit may need removal. Some produce requires blanching (placing in boiling water for a couple of minutes), such as apples, asparagus and green beans. Other fruits require heating or cooking before bottling (pears, quince).

Some fruit and other produce can be bottled in their juices or some syrup (typically a strong or concentrated sugar solution), while others in brine (e.g. tomatoes). Brine is a solution of salt that may vary from about 3 per cent (seawater) to 20 per cent (saturated salt solution).

Pack as much fruit or produce as you can pack into the jar, cover with water, brine or syrup, depending on what works best for that produce. Ensure no bubbles of air are trapped. Shaking, tapping the jar or a gentle stirring may dislodge air.

While you can leave some fruit and plant material without further treatment, many bottled fruits require sterilisation – heating or boiling water for about one hour to ensure all bacteria and fungi spores are killed and won't infect the bottled produce. The lids are quickly screwed on or clamped with spring clips as steam is escaping, driving air out. As the bottle cools, a partial vacuum is created, helping to further prevent micro-organisms from growing.

PROJECT

PICKLING

Pickling is bottling after fermentation or storing in brine (a strong salt solution) or vinegar. Fermentation is an anaerobic process where air is excluded, so many organisms cannot survive. This process does affect the taste, texture and flavour of the produce.

Sauerkraut is made using cabbage leaves, which are covered in brine and left to ferment.

Generally, because of the acidic conditions (pH = 5 or less) most bacteria are killed or at least their rate of reproduction is drastically slowed, so perishable goods can be preserved for many months. Natural fermentation (by lactic acid bacteria) produce the required acidity.

Pickling is easy to do, and here are some handy hints:

- ☑ Preparation – smaller vegetables (cherry tomatoes) are kept whole. Larger vegetables (cucumbers, carrots) are cut into slices or chunks.
- ☑ You don't need to add neat vinegar, so mix equal parts with water.
- ☑ While brine varies in salt concentration, try three tablespoons (50 grams) in one litre of water. You may have to heat a little to fully dissolve. This is approximately 5 per cent salt solution.
- ☑ Experiment with herbs to flavour, e.g. thyme, dill, rosemary, ginger and spices (coriander, peppercorns). Add small amounts of some of these to each jar or bottle of vegetables. For example, a twig of rosemary or thyme, one or two slices of ginger or three or four peppercorns or coriander seeds.

'Pickles' can be gherkins (a small West Indian cucumber) or strips of the common cucumber kept in vinegar.

PROJECT

RECIPES FOR EXCESS GARDEN PRODUCE

Try some of these easy recipes when you find yourself with an overabundance of certain crops. Jams and preserves make excellent gifts for students to take home to their families.

Some general materials you will need include:

JARS AND BOTTLES A selection of different sizes, with seals, will make your job a lot easier. Mason and Kilner jars (wide mouth, with screw lids), storage jars (clip top with rubber seal), plastic (PET) bottles and swing top bottles (with rubber Grolsch seal) are all required to preserve your products.

SUNDRY EQUIPMENT Cheesecloth, muslin, balance or scales. Muslin and cheesecloth are both fine cotton cloths (but do come in various mesh sizes), but any fine woven cotton material will work – even a tea-towel.

HYGIENE Cleanliness, at all times, is essential.

JAM

Most fruits utilise the same recipe to make jam. You could experiment with less sugar and add lime juice, or add two different fruits together. Some fruits have naturally high levels of pectin that make the jam 'set', but others require you to add a small amount of pectin or products such as 'jamsetta' or 'jam setting sugar'. It is best to experiment with a small trial yourself, before you let students make these products.

INGREDIENTS

- [x] 1 kg figs, raspberries or other berries, apricots, cherries or plums
- [x] 1 kg sugar*
- [x] water
- [x] juice of 1 lemon
- [x] pectin (to set jam)*

* You can buy a number of different brands of jam setting sugar from most supermarkets. These products contain both sugar and pectin.

METHOD

1. Chop fruit into slices or small chinks. Place in pot and just cover with water. Add sugar and pectin, and then heat and stir to dissolve.

2. You will need to stir every now and again to prevent burning of the mixture on the bottom of the pan.

3. To test whether the jam is ready to bottle, place a drop onto a cold plate. It should 'set'. If it still runs, keep heating the jam mixture.

PROJECT

APRICOT CHUTNEY

This is much fruitier than traditional chutneys, which often contain lemon juice, vinegar and a number of spices that make the garnish a little tart.

INGREDIENTS

- ☑ 1½ kg apricots (or peaches or mangoes)
- ☑ 500 g chopped onions
- ☑ 2 cups vinegar
- ☑ 750 g raw sugar
- ☑ 1 tsp salt
- ☑ 1 tsp mixed spice
- ☑ 1 tsp ground cloves
- ☑ 1 tsp curry powder

METHOD

1. Chop fruit up.
2. Combine all ingredients in large pot, stirring until sugar dissolves. Gently boil for 1 hour until chutney is thick.
3. Bottle and seal immediately.
4. Store in cool dark cupboard.

PROJECT

TOMATO RELISH

Tomato relish is a more savoury condiment that can be used as a substitute for tomato-based sauces.

INGREDIENTS

- [x] 1 kg tomatoes
- [x] 2 onions
- [x] 1 red chilli
- [x] 1 red capsicum
- [x] 1 tbs salt
- [x] 1½ cups raw sugar
- [x] 1½ cups cider vinegar
- [x] 2 tsp mustard powder
- [x] 1 tsp turmeric
- [x] 2 tsp tapioca starch

METHOD

1. Chop tomatoes, chilli, onions and capsicum into centimetre square pieces, and place in large bowl. Mix salt in and allow to stand for 2 hours.
2. Drain all liquid off. Put mixture into saucepan, add sugar, vinegar, mustard and turmeric and bring to boil. Cook for 30 minutes.
3. Mix the tapioca starch with a little bit of (extra) vinegar to make a paste. Add to the mixture and stir thoroughly. Boil for another 3 minutes (no more or mixture will stick to the pan). Spoon into sterilised jars.

GARLIC SALT

A simple change to make ordinary salt extraordinary. You can add 1 teaspoon of garlic powder (or any other herb powders) to every 10 teaspoons of salt to flavour it.

PROJECT

LEMON CURD

Great sweet filler for tarts, lemon meringue pies, with ice-cream, spread on toast – the list goes on. This recipe makes about 1½ cups of curd, which is also known as lemon butter.

INGREDIENTS

- [x] 2 eggs
- [x] ½ cup sugar
- [x] ¼ cup lemon juice (one large lemon)
- [x] 1 tbs grated lemon zest (from same lemon)
- [x] ½ cup butter in finely chopped pieces

METHOD

1. Place eggs, sugar, lemon juice and zest in a saucepan.
2. Heat gently and whisk continuously.
3. Whisk until curd becomes thick. Do not boil curd. Remove from heat and leave to cool. It should thicken further.

POWDERED LEMON

A good lemon tree will yield far too many lemons for a family to use or give away. Some lemons can be stored in a couple of practical ways.

Firstly, you can freeze them. But this does damage the tissue and when they are thawed out they don't look that great. They often expand and split during the freezing process, enabling juice to be lost.

Secondly, you can cut the lemons in slices and then dry in a dehydrator. Once dried, the slices can be stored in dark jars or paper bags until needed. They seem to keep the flavour well and when added to dishes the lemon flavour is evident.

Finally, the next step is to put the dried slices into a blender and grind into powder. Make sure you remove the seeds first! The lemon powder keeps well if it is kept dry, as long as

PART 3

GARDENING SKILLS

COLLECTING SEED FROM THE GARDEN

Seed saving is an important task. It enables you to use your collected seed to grow new plants. Once gathered, seeds need to be stored away from pest attack, harsh sunlight and damp conditions.

MATERIALS

- ☑ large paper bags, plastic bags
- ☑ elastic bands or garden tie wire
- ☑ labels
- ☑ recycled envelopes or small paper bags

METHOD

1. Identify plants that have maturing seed pods. Normally you should see pods or woody fruits becoming drier and harder, or turning from green to brown. Sometimes you can just pick ripe pods and remove the seeds, but often you will have to wait until the pods are mature.

2. Place a large plastic or paper bag over drying pods or fruits. Secure the bag opening by using an elastic band or tie wire, fixing it to the stem or branch.

3. Leave the bag for a few weeks, inspecting each week to see if seeds have fallen into the bag, the fruits or pods are splitting or are reasonably mature and dry.

4. Remove bag carefully, ensuring seeds don't fall out as you slip if off the branch. Separate the seeds from the 'chaff' – other plant material such as twigs, pod fragments and shells.

5. Store seeds in a small paper bag or envelope. Jars are suitable too, provided they are free of moisture. Label the seed bags with common name and variety, scientific name, date of collection or when stored, and location site of collection.

6. Use the seeds to produce new plants or for other activities in this book.

GARDENING SKILLS

SEED BOMBS

Seed bombs (or seed balls) are small spheres of clay and compost that contain seeds inside. The clay holds the ball together and protects the seed from adverse weather and predators, while the compost provides nutrition when the seed germinates. Both the clay and compost hold water to trigger germination. Seed bombs enable you to store seeds until they are needed, then you can throw them into revegetation areas and allow then to germinate when conditions are right.

MATERIALS

- ☑ clay – any colour, dry or damp
- ☑ seeds – any seeds of trees, vegetables or herbs that you want to plant. You will have greater success if you know that these types of seeds usually germinate easily
- ☑ compost – aged compost or good quality potting soil. This should be screened if coarse, as you only want fine compost material
- ☑ water

METHOD

1. Moisten clay (if required) and break off small chunks. Mould into small balls about 8 millimetres in diameter. The clay should not be sticky.

2. To each ball add 8 millimetres of compost or good quality soil (must contain organic matter). Vermicompost, or worm castings would be suitable too.

3. Mix these two ingredients well. The ball will be about 12 to 15 millimetres in size now. If the ball doesn't hold together then add a little more clay. Adjust the size to keep the ball no more than 1.5 centimetres in diameter. Balls that are between 10 to 15 millimetres work best. Do not make large seed bombs – sometimes the seeds cannot grow through all the clay.

4. Break open the seed bomb and insert one or two seeds (no more). Large seeds can be positioned in the middle of the ball while small seeds towards one outside edge. Too many seeds overcrowd the plants when they germinate.

5. Store the seed bombs in a cool, shaded area until you need them. The seed bombs will naturally air-dry, become lighter in colour and harden.

6. When you want to plant them or scatter somewhere, there are two options. To scatter, simply throw the balls into a revegetation area and let nature take its course. When the rains come, the balls absorb water and seeds will germinate. If the planting season is right for that seed, then soak the balls in a jar of water for ten to fifteen seconds – enough to moisten the balls well. Now you can plant or throw into the garden and wait for the shoots to emerge over the coming weeks.

GARDENING SKILLS

RESPROUTING VEGETABLES

Don't throw out your scraps just yet! Some vegetables can be re-sprouted to produce another round of food.

MATERIALS:

- ☑ a range of vegetables, such as carrot and beetroot tops, bases of celery and lettuce, onion, garlic bulb, potato
- ☑ toothpicks. Large vegetable parts may require skewers, which are more robust and can support more weight
- ☑ glass jars
- ☑ water

METHOD

1. Discuss with students the function of roots, leaves and stems. Guide students to understand that some parts of vegetables can be regrown to make additional food. For example, a carrot top can be placed in water and while it will not produce a carrot (swollen root) it will produce leafy greens which are edible. A potato and a sweet potato (these are not related) will produce new roots, a stem and then leaves to make a new plant.

2. Students will have an opportunity to grow their own plants, but you may choose to do this as a whole class activity unless you have lots of vegetables and equipment. Each small group could set-up one vegetable.

3. Generally a vegetable part is suspended in a jar of water. Three or four toothpicks are used to secure the sweet potato or other vegetable. The toothpicks are placed evenly into the flesh about 2 or more centimetres from the bottom or exposed end (if you are using a cut potato or sweet potato). Onions might just sit on the rim and lettuce or celery bases may need to sit in a bowl rather than a glass.

4. Students should then fill a jar with water and rest the vegetable part so that the toothpicks sit on the rim and the exposed end of the vegetable lies in the water at a depth of around 1 to 4 centimetres.

5. Over the next few weeks, students should begin to see new growth – it may be roots, leaves or a sprout or two growing from the top.

PART 4
THE GARDEN ENVIRONMENT

Every garden is affected by environmental factors that influence the lives of the plants and animals within it. These can include climate, soil type and the particular plants and animals that are present.

The activities in this section allow students to understand the relationships between organisms and their environment, how they interact with other species and how they have adapted to respond to different environmental conditions.

TEACHER'S NOTES:

Observing life cycles in the garden	88
Interactions in the garden	91
Adaptations in the garden	97
Seed dispersal	101
Seasons and change	110

INVESTIGATIONS:

Animal interactions simulation	92
Observing adaptations of climbing plants	98
Design a seed	102
Hidden colours	111

PROJECTS:

Fruit fly trap	108
Exploring plant dyes	113

GARDENING SKILLS:

Pest management	105

Teacher's Notes

Observing Life Cycles in the Garden

A life cycle describes the sequence of changes that an organism undergoes as it grows to maturity. Every type of organism has a life cycle – it's nature's way of ensuring new organisms are made so that their crucial role in the environment continues.

Humans and other animals usually grow larger and stronger as they grow, but many insects (as well as animals such as frogs) undergo more striking changes on their journey to adulthood. This process is called **metamorphosis**, and often involves the transformation of an animal's physical characteristics, as well as other changes in their diet and behaviour.

The diagram below shows the life cycle of a butterfly. As you can see, there are four distinct stages to their life cycle. A caterpillar hatches from the egg (the larval stage) and eats nearby leaves. After a period of growth, it will spin itself a chrysalis (the pupal stage) before emerging in its adult state as a butterfly. The butterfly will use its new wings to visit and feed on the nectar of flowers, and eventually go on to lay eggs of its own, starting the cycle again for a new generation of butterflies.

Continued...

Teacher's Notes

Frog-Friendly Gardens

Introducing frogs to your garden can be a fascinating way for students to observe animal life cycles up close. Frogs are also good bio-indicators, as they are susceptible to poisons, poor water quality, herbicides and changing environmental conditions. The population of frogs in your garden can therefore be a great measure for the overall health of the garden environment.

Frogs will naturally come into garden ponds if the conditions are right. You are not allowed to move frogs or tadpoles from one area to another, nor catch them in national parks or other wetland areas.

Frogs need habitat, such as wetlands plants (e.g. *Juncus*, *Baumea*, *Isolepis*, *Eleocharis* and *Schoenoplectus* spp.) to hide in and water to breed in. Ponds are best built in mostly shade areas of the garden as direct sunlight can cause overgrowth of algae which is difficult to control when frogs are present. Some sunlight is essential to trigger frog breeding and for plants to grow. Maintain any floating plants so that water cover is only about one-half to two-thirds. Open water is important for frogs.

Frogs also need plenty of shelter, so be sure to place an old flowerpot or hollowed log nearby. Plants such as dianella, lomandra and iris can be planted in the wet fringe around the pond. Students can research what plants attract insects so that the frogs have easy meals while they wait for insect life in the pond to build up.

Continued...

Teacher's Notes

MEALWORMS

Mealworms are easy to keep in the classroom and are a simple way for students to observe the life cycle of an insect. Mealworms are the larval stage of a common beetle, *Tenebrio molitor*, which is found throughout the world. They breed rapidly and can be used as fishing bait, and food for frogs and chickens, fish and lizards. Specimens are easy to obtain from scientific and school suppliers.

Once you have bought either mealworms or the adult beetles, keep then in an ice-cream container or similar plastic box. Half fill the container with wheat bran, oatmeal or dry, crushed wheat-based breakfast cereals. Mealworms require a moist environment, so place a damp cloth or paper towel on the surface and re-soak this occasionally. You can also place a slice of apple, potato or other fruits or vegetables on the surface once in a while. Mealworms do not like bright light or hot or very cold conditions, so try to keep them warm and away from direct sunlight. Humidity increases their reproductive rate, but normal classroom humidity is sufficient. Only in dry climates should you endeavour to increase humidity around the mealworm population.

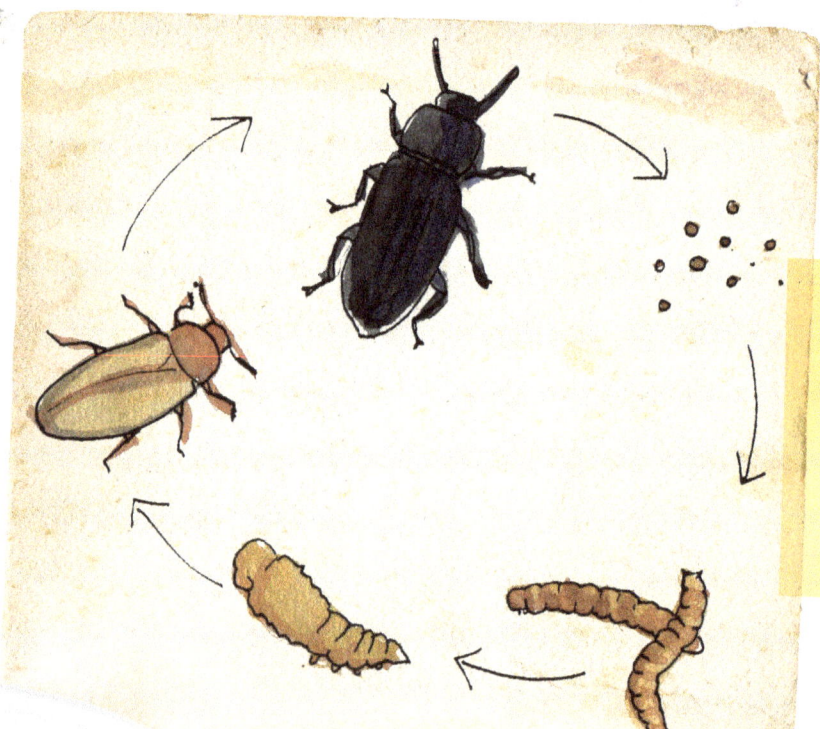

Students should be able to witness all stages of their life cycle and observe the various forms as they change.

Students can either draw or photograph the stages of insect metamorphosis and record how long it takes to change from one stage to another. Some beetles may fly away, but enough should stay around to breed and start their cycle all over again.

Students can also note the structural features of the mealworm as it passes through each stage, such as the number of legs (including the larval mealworm), body parts and antennae. They can also investigate the burrowing behaviour, and the effect of light (torchlight beam), touch, wind (blow through a straw), and other stimuli (water, chemicals – lavender, rosemary or similar oils) on its movements.

Teacher's Notes

Interactions in the Garden

All living things require adequate food and shelter in order to survive in their environment. Both animals and plants frequently interact with each other to help them fulfil these basic needs.

Plants are producers. They create food for themselves with the help of sunlight and nutrients in the soil.

Animals are consumers. They are unable to make their own food and must rely on the nutrients found in plants and other animals to survive. Animals that eat other animals are carnivores, while herbivores feed on plants. An omnivore is an animal that eats both animals and plants.

Mould, fungi and soil-based creatures, such as earthworms, are decomposers. They feed on dead organic matter, which is broken down over time, returning nutrients to the soil to be used by plants.

When organisms in the same environment have similar needs, they must compete with each other for the limited resources available. Competition between two species can cause one or both to die out. It is therefore vital that an ecosystem contains the right balance of producers, consumers and decomposers. A healthy environment generally contains more decomposers and producers than consumers. An abundance of plants ensures that food is readily available for herbivores to thrive and multiply, which in turn attracts larger carnivores to the area and keeps the herbivore population from becoming too numerous and consuming too many of the plants.

While many interactions between species are brief, and often deadly, other, more long-lasting relationships can be formed. Symbiosis refers to the ongoing interactions between two species. Symbiotic relationships can benefit one or both species involved.

MUTUALISM is a symbiotic relationship where both organisms benefit. A bee and a flowering plant is an example of mutualism. The bee feeds on the flower's nectar and gathers pollen to make honey, while the flowers rely on the bees to spread their pollen to other flowers so that they can produce seeds.

A tick is a parasite – it feeds on other living things

PARASITISM refers to interactions in which only one species benefits. A parasite is an organism that lives on or inside another living thing (the host) to use as a source of food. Common parasites include small animals like ticks and fleas, but can also include plants such as mistletoe. Parasites do not often cause the death of the host, but many parasites can be a source of irritation and can even cause serious illness.

COMMENSALISM is the third type of symbiosis. In these relationships, one organism benefits but the other is unharmed. It is a one-sided symbiotic relationship. Spiders spin webs in plants, hermit crabs live in discarded mollusc shells and many birds travel alongside sheep and cows as they graze on plants to reveal insects which the birds eat.

Symbiosis Type	Benefit to Species 1	Benefit to Species 2
Mutualism	✓	✓
Parasitism	✓	✗
Commensalism	✓	–

When working in the garden, it is important to consider how our decisions can affect the existing relationships between the species that live there. Seemingly small changes can result in negative consequences. For example, using chemical pesticides may prevent certain insects from attacking your plants, but can inadvertently cause the death of beneficial species. This can disrupt the food supply of predators, resulting in a reduction in their numbers, or disappearance from the garden altogether until the insects return.

PART 4

INVESTIGATION

ANIMAL INTERACTIONS SIMULATION

In this simulation, small groups will model various animal interactions to determine their relationship with each other.

MATERIALS

For each group:

- ☑ coloured counters, or similar materials (12 each of blue, green, red and yellow), placed into bowls
- ☑ plastic cups, labelled 1, 2, 3 and 4
- ☑ plastic spoons, enough for each student
- ☑ photocopy of instruction cards on page 94, cut out and given to each group
- ☑ worksheet: animal interactions simulation (available on page 95), one for each student

METHOD

1. Discuss with students how animals interact in the garden (see notes on page 91), taking particular note of competition and forms of symbiosis.

2. Ask students if they know what a simulation is. Explain that scientists often run simulations to help them understand how things work, and that the students are going to run a simulation to demonstrate how animals interact with each other.

3. Arrange students into groups of four. Give each group a bowl of counters, and each member a worksheet, a labelled cup, plastic spoon and instruction card for their species.

4. Explain that this simulation has four rounds. In each round, students will take on the role of a different animal species. Their labelled cups will indicate which species they are and which instruction card they need. (i.e. cup 1 receives species 1 card, etc.)

5. Explain that the counters represent the food available in an environment. At the beginning of each round, students must read their individual instruction card to find out what they will need to do to survive. On 'go', all group members will begin using their plastic spoons to transfer the counters they need from the bowl to their cup. They may only transfer one counter at a time. The round ends when players are unable to gather any more of the counters they need.

   Note: You may wish to explain to students that this is a simulation, not a game, and that not surviving a round does not mean they have 'lost'. Some rounds are harder for certain species and easier for others.

6. At the end of each round, students should count up the food they have gathered and see if their species survived the round. They should then discuss what kind of relationship each species had with the other and record this on their worksheet. They will then place the counters back into the bowl to begin the next round.

7. Once all four rounds have been completed, students can then experiment with the simulation by changing the number of counters available in the bowl and playing through each round again to see how this affects their interactions with each other.

Continued...

INVESTIGATION

EXTENSIONS

- Groups of students can try designing their own simulations for another group to model. They should attempt to include at least two kinds of interactions in their simulation.
- Students can learn more about animal interactions by using one of the following online simulations:
- Younger Students: *Food Chain Challenge*

    https://www.bbc.co.uk/bitesize/articles/z93vdxs
- Older Students: *Feed the Dingo*, *Make a Mangrove* or *Jungle Jeopardy*, found at

    https://pbskids.org/plumlanding/games/index.html

ACTIVITY SHEET
INSTRUCTION CARDS

Cut out each card and give one to each group member

SPECIES 1
Round 1:
Only eats green food.
You need at least 6 pieces to survive.
Round 2:
Eats any colour of food but you can only take food from other species' cups.
You need at least 6 pieces to survive
Round 3:
Eats any colour of food, but you may only pick up blue food.
You need 2 of each colour to survive.
Round 4:
Eats blue and green food.
The red food is harmful. Before gathering your own food, you must first collect all the red food and place it outside the bowl.
You need at least 6 pieces to survive.

SPECIES 2
Round 1:
Only eats blue food
You need at least 6 pieces to survive.
Round 2:
Eats blue and green food.
You need at least 6 pieces to survive.
Round 3:
Eats any colour of food, but you may only pick up green food.
You need 2 of each colour to survive.
Round 4:
Only eats blue food.
The red food is harmful. Before gathering your own food, you must first collect all the red food and place it outside the bowl.
You need at least 6 pieces to survive.

SPECIES 3
Round 1:
Only eats blue food
You need at least 6 pieces to survive.
Round 2:
Eats green and red food.
You need at least 6 pieces to survive.
Round 3:
Eats any colour of food, but you may only pick up red food.
You need 2 of each colour to survive.
Round 4:
Only eats red food. You can only pick up red food when they are placed outside of the bowl.
You need at least 6 pieces to survive.

SPECIES 4
Round 1:
Only eats green food
You need at least 6 pieces to survive.
Round 2:
Eats blue and yellow food.
You need at least 6 pieces to survive.
Round 3:
Eats any colour of food, but you may only pick up yellow food.
You need 2 of each colour to survive.
Round 4:
Only eats red food. You can only pick up red food when they are placed outside of the bowl.
You need at least 6 pieces to survive.

ACTIVITY SHEET
ANIMAL INTERACTIONS SIMULATION

DIRECTIONS

At the end of each round, write down the relationship between each species. The word bank below will remind you of the different types of animal interactions.

COMPETITION   **PARASITISM**   **MUTUALISM**

COMMENSALISM   **NO RELATIONSHIP**

Round 1: Name the relationship between:

Species 1 and 2: _____   Species 1 and 4: _____

Species 1 and 3: _____   Species 2 and 4: _____

Species 2 and 3: _____   Species 3 and 4: _____

Did all species survive? _____

What made survival difficult during this round? _____

_____

_____

Round 2: Name the relationship between:

Species 1 and 2: _____   Species 1 and 4: _____

Species 1 and 3: _____   Species 2 and 4: _____

Species 2 and 3: _____   Species 3 and 4: _____

Did all species survive? _____

What made survival difficult during this round? _____

_____

_____

Continued...

ACTIVITY SHEET
ANIMAL INTERACTIONS SIMULATION

COMPETITION   PARASITISM   MUTUALISM

COMMENSALISM   NO RELATIONSHIP

Round 3: Name the relationship between:

Species 1 and 2:_____   Species 1 and 4:_____

Species 1 and 3:_____   Species 2 and 4:_____

Species 2 and 3:_____   Species 3 and 4:_____

Did all species survive? _____

What made survival difficult during this round? _____
_____
_____

Round 4: Name the relationship between:

Species 1 and 2:_____   Species 1 and 4:_____

Species 1 and 3:_____   Species 2 and 4:_____

Species 2 and 3:_____   Species 3 and 4:_____

Did all species survive? _____

What made survival difficult during this round? _____
_____
_____

PART 4

Teacher's notes

Adaptations in the Garden

Adaptations are features of an organism that allow it to survive in its environment. They generally fall into one of three categories:

STRUCTURAL ADAPTATIONS refer to an organism's physical characteristics, such as size, height or means of defence. These include the tusks of elephants, the waxy reflective leaves of eucalypts, and the long tongue and spines of the echidna.

FUNCTIONAL ADAPTATIONS are the features which help an organism's body work more efficiently. This includes temperature regulation in mammals and birds, making urine to regulate the water levels in our body and the self-pruning of gum tree branches when water is scarce.

BEHAVIOURAL ADAPTATIONS refer to the instinctual actions of an organism. This might include hibernation, annual migration and swarming.

Many adaptations enable organisms to tolerate changes to their environment. For example, desert plants must survive in areas of low rainfall and temperature extremes, so they possess a range of adaptations, such as waxy leaves to reflect excess light, deep roots to access water, organs that store water and leaves that are curled to prevent water loss.

Adaptations in the garden are easy to spot. You can find plants that have large leaves to make more food; deep roots so that they can better absorb water and minerals; seeds that are like parachutes that float in the wind; and storage organs that can be used to provide the plant with nutrients during adverse conditions. Use the worksheet on page 100 to help students identify the adaptations of plants in the school garden and surrounding area.

Extensive root system

Cactus stems are photosynthetic – they can produce food just like leaves

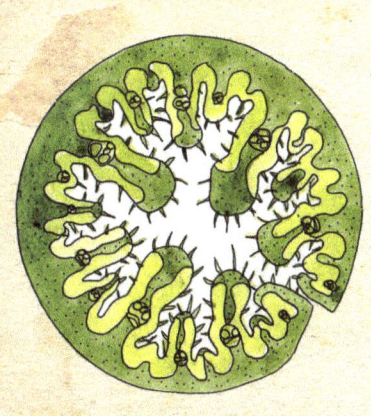

Some leaves curl themselves up to protect themselves in hot weather

Some leaves have hair on their surface

Many leaves are reduced in size and become spines

INVESTIGATION

OBSERVING ADAPTATIONS OF CLIMBING PLANTS

In this activity, students will build a simple trellis and observe how it supports the growth of a climbing plant.

BACKGROUND NOTES

Climbing plants have unique adaptations that enable them to grow upwards and successfully compete for sunlight. They have specialised organs called tendrils which can move and wrap around structures, pulling the plant upwards. These tendrils have high tensile strength and can contract or unwind to drag the main body of the plant in the required direction.

MATERIALS

- ☑ a vine to display, either an indoor potted vine, or a vine on the school grounds
- ☑ sweet (or other) pea seedlings, one for each group or student
- ☑ time-lapse video of climbing plant, such as the one here: https://www.youtube.com/watch?v=dTljalVseTc (short, succinct) and a longer (older) but more scientific discussion at https://www.youtube.com/watch?v=n3MAOlBOWgE.
- ☑ 1 metre fencing wire, one length for each group/student
- ☑ ice-cream stick or other label for plants

    Option: other materials for alternative trellis – lengths of wood or bamboo, string or wire, cable ties etc.

PART 4

Continued...

INVESTIGATION

METHOD

1. Show students an example of a vine, especially if it has attached to a frame or trellis. Ask, 'How is this plant different from others?' *It is attached to another object, it doesn't stand up straight etc.*

2. Point out the vine's tendrils, and ask students to see if they can find more examples. What do you think a tendril is for? *Holding on to things.* Show a time lapse video of this process.

3. Tell students 'We are going to build something that a vine can hold on to. It is called a trellis.'

4. Show some examples of trellises, either pictures online or ones that already exist in the garden. Explain that students will build a supporting frame or trellis from fencing wire.

5. Allow time for students to construct their trellis using the materials provided. Bend 1 metre of fencing wire to make a series of small loops along its length. You might need to use a pair of pliers. Make the first loop at 30 centimetres and a loop every 10 centimetres thereafter.

6. Once the trellis has been constructed, it is time to plant. Put a seedling in a 1 litre pot filled with good soil. Add vertical trellis frame. Label their seedling with an ice-cream stick with their name on it.

7. Students can then use the planting diary on page 138 to track the growth of their plant and record any observations. Particular attention should be given to the growth and action of the tendrils.

8. Students should periodically check the progress of their vine to ensure that plants are watered and cared for, and their trellis is working effectively. Examine how tendrils wrap around the wire to support the plant. They can also take photographs of tendril attachment and the plant growth.

EXTENSION

Student can use the worksheet on page 100 to observe other plant adaptations around the garden.

ACTIVITY SHEET 🛒

PLANT ADAPTATIONS

DIRECTIONS

Visit the plants that are growing in the school garden, or on the school grounds. Choose two plants and make some observations below.

PLANT NAME: _____

LEAVES: HAIRY ☐   SHINY ☐   WAXY ☐   SPIKY ☐   FRAGRANT ☐

OTHER OBSERVATIONS: _____

FLOWERS: SMALL ☐   LARGE ☐   SCENTED ☐   COLOUR: _____

OTHER OBSERVATIONS: _____

STEMS: THORNS ☐   HAIR ☐   BARK ☐   SAP ☐

OTHER OBSERVATIONS: _____

PLANT NAME: _____

LEAVES: HAIRY ☐   SHINY ☐   WAXY ☐   SPIKY ☐   FRAGRANT ☐

OTHER OBSERVATIONS: _____

FLOWERS: SMALL ☐   LARGE ☐   SCENTED ☐   COLOUR: _____

OTHER OBSERVATIONS: _____

STEMS: THORNS ☐   HAIR ☐   BARK ☐   SAP ☐

OTHER OBSERVATIONS: _____

PART 4

Teacher's Notes

Seed Dispersal

When flowering plants mature, they make seeds. As the mortality rate of seeds is high, many plants produce large numbers of seeds so that a few can survive and grow into new plants.

Plants rely on a number of strategies to transport their seeds to new areas and away from the parent plants. This process is called seed dispersal. There are five main methods of dispersal:

WIND: Some seeds are small and light and can be blown by wind to new areas where they can grow. Winged seeds have feather-like structures that cause them to spiral around and slowly drift towards the ground, further away from the parent tree.

WATER: Some seeds have an air pocket that allows them to float in water. Flowing water carries the seeds to other areas. The seeds of water lilies, palm trees and coconut trees can be carried great distances by water currents.

EXPLOSIVE MECHANISMS: Some plants have pods that can split or explode, ejecting the seeds as far away as possible from the parent plant. Many wattle trees (*Acacia* species) as well as common garden plants, such as geraniums, use explosive mechanisms for seed dispersal.

GRAVITY: Gravity can also contribute to seed dispersal. Some seeds are large and heavy and have a rounded shape, which allows them to roll away from the parent tree, especially if the trees are found on sloped ground. Apples and coconuts are examples of fruits that use gravity for their dispersal.

ANIMALS AND HUMANS: Some seeds have hooks and burrs so that they attach to an animal's fur or skin. Other plants produce edible fruit that contains seeds. Animals and birds eat the fruit and drop their waste, containing the seeds, in new areas. In drier areas, ants play an important role in seed dispersal. They carry seeds away to their nest, feed their young some of the external seed coat and then discard the rest of the intact seed. After a while seeds germinate into new plants.

Humans are also seed dispersers. Studies have shown that seeds caught in their shoes may be dispersed five kilometres away, while those carried on clothes typically only 250 metres. Human transport of plants from one region to another or one country to another allows seeds to grow in completely different environments.

INVESTIGATION

DESIGN A SEED

In this activity, students will observe the structure of various seeds and predict how they might be dispersed. They will then design and build their own seed dispersal system based on one or two modes of dispersal.

MATERIALS

- ☑ a collection of different types of seeds, **or** copies of the 'seed dispersal' activity sheet on page 103
- ☑ magnifying glasses
- ☑ materials for constructing seed models, including copies of the 'design a seed' activity sheet on page 104
- ☑ a variety of different types of beads (to represent seeds)

SOME SUGGESTED MATERIALS

- ☑ craft supplies (paper, cardboard, glue, pipe cleaners etc.)
- ☑ feathers
- ☑ packing foam pieces
- ☑ office supplies (paper clips, rubber bands etc.)
- ☑ small boxes
- ☑ cardboard tubes

METHOD

1. Explain to students that seeds usually try to move as far away from the parent plant as possible. Discuss the different means by which plants disperse their seeds (see teacher's notes on page 101).

2. Hand out a collection of different seeds and a magnifying glass to each student or group. On a piece of paper or in their books, they should draw each seed in detail, noting any structures they find interesting. Finally, they should decide the mode by which the seed travels. If you are unable to provide seeds, use the provided activity sheet on page 103. Discuss findings as a class, ensuring that students back up their guesses with evidence.

3. Explain to students that scientists often create models to show how something works. Students will choose one or several beads to represent their seeds. They will then design, create and test a method for dispersing their seeds.

4. Students should first design their model using part 1 of the activity sheet on page 104. They may then begin building, testing and improving their model for as long as time allows.

5. Students can then participate in a 'gallery walk' in which students' seeds are displayed at their desks for their classmates, who will try to guess the means of dispersal. Individual students can then demonstrate their models to the class. (For demonstrating animal dispersal, bring in a few fluffy soft toys, or a woollen article of clothing.)

PART 4

ACTIVITY SHEET
SEED DISPERSAL

Flowering plants produce seeds that have adaptations to give them the best chance of spreading to other areas. Examine the drawings of the following seeds and decide whether they are dispersed by wind, water, animal or explosive mechanisms. Discuss your answers with the class.

ACTIVITY SHEET
DESIGN A SEED

1. Create a labelled sketch of your model below.

How my seed(s) will travel: _____

Materials I need to make this model: _____

2. Have a look at your classmates' seed models. Draw some of them below and guess how their seed travels. Label the features of the seed that helped in your guess.

PART 4

_____   _____   _____

Life in a Garden by Ross Mass | Reproducible

GARDENING SKILLS

PEST MANAGEMENT

Pest control is an important part of any garden. The notes below outline some of the general principles for maintaining good garden health and some of the techniques students can adopt as part of an environmentally friendly pest-management strategy.

- ☑ **DEVELOP A SUSTAINABLE POLYCULTURE.** Planting a variety of plants such as scented herbs amongst your vegetables confuses pests. Pests recognise plants by colour, shape or smell so if the vegetables are hidden by other plants nearby, pests cannot locate and attack. You can also use plant competition to control weeds. For example, pine needles inhibit weed seed germination.

- ☑ **HAVE A DIVERSITY OF STRATEGIES.** Use biological, chemical, cultural and physical. Biological control encourages predators to attack pests, and this is probably the most useful strategy to control pest numbers. Sometimes you just have to pick snails from cabbages (mechanical), sometimes cleaning up fallen fruit helps control fly numbers (cultural), and at other times some mild chemical sprays deter pests (chemical).

- ☑ **ENCOURAGE PREDATORS.** Often the problem of too many pests is actually an issue of too few predators. In nature, the predator cycle follows the pest cycle. Sometimes you just have to wait a few days for predators to appear, so don't panic when aphids cover the lemon tree. While you can initially respond with a light detergent spray, if you have host plants for predators in the garden soon you may see hoverflies and ladybugs hard at work.

- ☑ **DON'T ALLOW ANY '-ICIDES' NEAR YOUR GARDEN.** Try to minimise harmful chemicals such as insecticides, pesticides, fungicides and herbicides. These may often kill beneficial insects as well as pests.

- ☑ **NURTURE THE SOIL.** The soil is the key. Healthy soil means healthy plants, so focus on growing soil in the garden by adding lots of compost, mulch and amendments as required.

GARDENING SKILLS

ORGANIC SPRAYS FOR PEST CONTROL

These sprays are relatively easy to make in a classroom, although some recipes do require heating, so a science laboratory or kitchen classroom would be ideal. Ensure students wear safety glasses when heating any solutions and disposable gloves when handling plants and materials that can contain irritants. Some of these sprays repel insects and other animals, while others help ward off disease.

Some recipes require the addition of vegetable oil. This helps the solution stick to the plant parts and also helps to affect the pests themselves. Spray plants as a treatment strategy or as a preventative measure, but try to only spray on infected parts of plants.

GARLIC SPRAY

Garlic spray makes a good general pesticide. Add four finely chopped cloves of garlic to 1 litre of water and allow it to stand overnight. Mix in a tablespoon of soap flakes to help the spray adhere to plants.

PLANT INSECTICIDE

Mix a cake of soap flakes in 2 litres of water. Heat until boiling and pour in 3 litres of kerosene. An emulsion is formed. For scale insects dilute 10 times with water; for other insects dilute 15 times.

CHAMOMILE TEA

Chamomile tea can help deter mould forming on plants in damp areas. Steep a handful of fresh flowers in 1 litre of boiling water. Strain the tea and use immediately.

Continued...

GARDENING SKILLS

WORMWOOD SPRAY

Place around 25 grams of dried wormwood leaves in a pot and cover with a litre of water. Allow to simmer for around 30 minutes and then set aside to cool. Use only on mature plants for larger pests such as caterpillars, moths and aphids.

PYRETHRUM

A natural insecticide, pyrethrum flower head can be dried and ground to produce a powder that can be applied directly to the garden, or made into a spray by combining 30 grams of flower heads with 50 millilitres of methylated spirits and diluted in 18 litres of water.

COFFEE SPRAY

Coffee repels slugs and snails. Use one part strong coffee (not instant coffee) to 10 parts warm water – about one tablespoon in a cup of water. Stir to dissolve, allow to cool and spray over plants that slugs and snails are known to attack.

SOAP SPRAY

Add 2 millilitres of detergent or a teaspoon of soap flakes and two teaspoons of vegetable oil to one litre of water. Gently mix so solution doesn't foam excessively. Spray onto plant leaves to deter soft-bodied pests such as aphids, caterpillars and mealybugs. The oil will smother the pests.

FUNGICIDE SPRAY

Dilute half a cup of milk with two cups of water. Spray onto leaves to reduce the incidence of powdery mildew and other soots and moulds.

A stronger fungicide spray can be made by mixing 1 teaspoon of sodium hydrogen carbonate (bicarbonate of soda) with 1 teaspoon of vegetable oil in 2 litres of water.

RHUBARB SPRAY

Simmer a kilogram of rhubarb leaves for 30 minutes to make a spray for deterring small insects.

PART 4

PROJECT

MAKE A FRUIT FLY TRAP

Fruit flies are serious pests in Australia. There are two different species: the Mediterranean Fruit Fly (medfly) can be found in Western Australia, while the Queensland Fruit Fly (Qfly) is common throughout the Northern Territory, Queensland, New South Wales and in some parts of Victoria. Qflies are considered more dangerous because they attack a greater variety of fruit plants, often before the fruit has ripened for harvesting.

These simple traps can help mitigate any problem pests. They allow flies to enter through small holes in the lid or side. Once inside, they cannot easily escape.

MATERIALS

- ☑ soft drink or water bottle (wash or remove any labels)
- ☑ bait solution (see recipes below)
- ☑ string
- ☑ drill, bit or soldering iron

BAIT SOLUTIONS TO TRY

1. **YEAST SOLUTION.** Add 80 grams sugar ($1/3$ cup) and 1.5 grams dry brewer's yeast ($1/3$ sachet) to 920 millilitres water. Mix to dissolve sugar. Keep the solution warm to ensure growth of yeast.

2. **PUNGENT SOLUTION.** Add 5 millilitres vanilla essence and 20 millilitres household ammonia in 1 litre water.

3. **PROTEIN SOLUTION.** To 1 litre water add 50 grams brown sugar, 1 sachet (5 grams) dry yeast and 1 tablespoon (20 grams) vegemite (or marmite – these are both yeast extracts). Protein baits tend to attract more females.

4. **SWEET APPLE CIDER VINEGAR.** Add a tablespoon of honey to 500 millilitres apple cider vinegar (you can often buy honey apple cider vinegar already as a solution). You can make this neat (no dilution) or mix 50 per cent with water.

   Options: adding a few drops of liquid detergent breaks the surface tension of the solution and flies cannot stay on top of the liquid. Use honey, maple syrup or molasses as alternatives to sugar.

Continued...

PROJECT

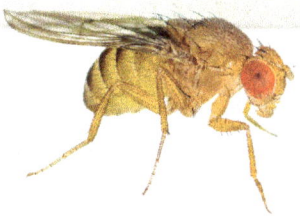

METHOD

1. Drill, punch or burn (with soldering iron) at least one hole in the side of the bottle (around 6–8 millimetres in diameter.) You can also experiment with two holes made in either side, and have students compare the results.

2. Place a small amount of bait solution in the bottle. Fill to about 3 centimetres.

Some alternative fruit fly trap designs to try.

3. Tie string around the neck of the bottle and hang in a tree in the garden. Ideally, these should be hung about 1.5 metres above the ground.

4. Check on the traps each day. Eventually they may need emptying and refilling with fresh bait solution. It is important to dispose of any bait solution away from the garden area, so that flies are not drawn to the liquid.

Students can try this method as well. Cut up some soft fruit and place in a clear glass bowl. Cover with stretch plastic wrap. Place one or two holes (well apart) in the plastic sheet. Leave in a sheltered (from sun) place. You will probably also attract vinegar fly (*Drosophila* spp.). Vinegar flies feed on the yeasts that decay the fruit and are often wrongly thought of as fruit flies.

Teacher's Notes

Seasons and Change

A garden changes as seasons change. The weather is closely connected to the life cycle of a plant. Plants flower and bear fruit at different times of the year. Many common vegetables and herbs are annuals, living only for one year. As the seasons change they produce seeds and die soon afterwards. See the planting guide on page 118 for more information on winter and summer crops.

Deciduous trees provide plenty of shade during summer, but begin to lose their leaves and become dormant as the day and night temperatures fall. They store food and nutrients in their stems, branches and roots to help them survive the cold winter months. When the daytime temperatures start to rise again, the plants burst into life, producing new leaves and growing taller.

Changes in Leaves

One of the most striking changes in the garden occurs in autumn, when leaves begin to change colour from green to shades of yellow, orange and red. These colourful pigments are composed of chemicals such as chlorophyll (green), carotene and carotenoids (yellow) and xanthophylls (red). Chlorophyll is responsible for photosynthesis – the process by which a plant produces food with the help of sunlight. The other pigments aid in photosynthesis by absorbing different wavelengths of light. As winter approaches, a deciduous tree begins reabsorbing nutrients from the leaves to store for the spring. This process causes the chlorophyll to break down, allowing other pigments to become visible.

PART 4

INVESTIGATION

HIDDEN COLOURS

This activity uses chromatography to investigate some of the plant pigments that are found in leaves. As the pigment travels up the paper, the chemicals separate into a coloured band, revealing the hidden pigments that are usually invisible to the naked eye.

PART 1

MATERIALS

- ☑ black textas, one for each child or group (ideally a variety of brands)
- ☑ filter paper or paper towel – cut into strips to fit inside test tube or jar, and long enough so that they can be removed
- ☑ plastic cup – one for each group
- ☑ water

METHOD

1. Ask students why they think leaves change colour as it get colder. Tell them that they will perform an experiment that might help them answer this question.

2. Have students use their black texta to make a large dot around 3 centimetres from the bottom of their paper strip.

3. Add around 5 centimetres of water to the cup.

4. Place the strip vertically inside the cup, so that the black dot is sitting inside the cup (but above the water level) and fold the top of the strip over the rim. Watch the water climb up the strip.

5. As the water rises up the strip, it will carry some of the ink with it, causing the pigments in the ink to separate and revealing the hidden pigments of the texta (these are often shades of blue and red).

6. Students may now be able to develop a hypothesis about the colour in leaves and other plant parts. The colours had always been there, but are hidden by the green chlorophyll in the plant. Tell students that we can test this hypothesis by performing a similar experiment with green leaves.

PART 4

Continued...

INVESTIGATION

PART 2

MATERIALS

PART 2
- ☑ methylated spirits
- ☑ several green leaves for each group
- ☑ 150 ml long test tubes or plastic vials
- ☑ filter paper or paper towel – cut into strips to fit inside test tube or vial, and long enough so that they can be removed
- ☑ eye dropper

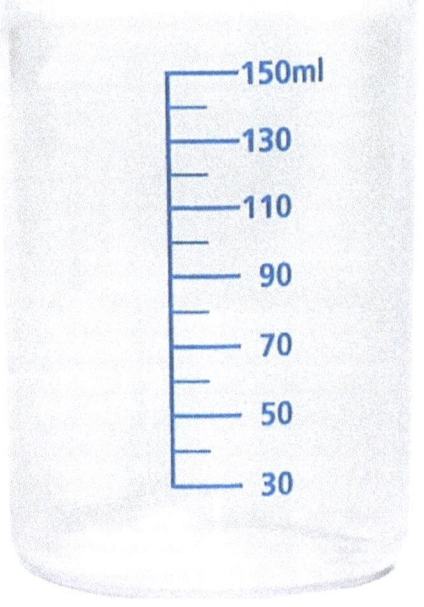

METHOD

1. Have each group cut five to 10 green leaves into small pieces and place these in a jar. Each jar should only contain one type of leaf.
2. Add 10 millilitres methylated spirits. Do not add too much as the resulting pigment solution will be weak.
3. Set aside for at least a few hours and push any plant material down so that it is below the liquid surface.
4. Use an eye dropper to place one drop of solution on a 2 centimetre strip of paper towel or filter paper, about 3 centimetres from the bottom.
5. Allow the pigment drop to dry before adding another pigment drop on top of the first. Repeat this a few times, in order to get a concentrated sample of pigment on the paper.
6. When the drops are completely dry place 2 centimetres of methylated spirits in a clean test tube or glass jar. Carefully lower the paper strip into the liquid, so that the pigment is at the bottom and the top is folded over the rim of the jar or tube.
7. The liquid will rise up the paper, dissolving pigments and carrying them towards the top. When the paper is wet near the top, remove it from the test tube, mark the level with a pencil and allow to dry. Use the pencil to mark or circle the various colours on the paper. Record the colours alongside these markings.

PROJECT
EXPLORING PLANT DYES

Plant dyes have been used for thousands of years to colour and decorate fabrics. Here are a few simple activities for students to produce their own colourful creations.

GENERAL MATERIALS

- ☑ various coloured plant parts (see below for some suggestions)
- ☑ white fabric – cotton, wool, silk or other linen material – old sheets, t-shirts
- ☑ kitchen strainer, cheesecloth or old stocking, wooden spoon

Optional: alum (aluminium potassium sulphate) or cream of tartar (potassium hydrogen tartrate). These are used as mordants, which 'fix' the dye to the material.

COLOUR	PLANT PARTS
Blue	Elderberry fruits, red/purple cabbage leaves
Yellow	Flowers of calendula, chamomile, dandelion, marigolds, sunflower. Brown onion skins (modified leaves), pomegranate skins/peel
Green	Leaves of spinach, cabbage and carrots
Orange	Tumeric
Brown	Coffee grounds, red onion skins
Purple	Grapes (dark), mulberries, purple carrots

Continued...

PROJECT

POUNDED FLOWER PRINTS

This activity transfers pigments directly to fabric, creating colourful plant patterns to decorate clothing or make prints to frame later.

MATERIALS

- ☑ rubber mallet (although a plain hammer will do)
- ☑ fresh leaves, flowers, or both. Try various eucalypt leaves as these are common trees throughout Australia
- ☑ thick cardboard
- ☑ safety goggles/glasses
- ☑ masking tape
- ☑ clothing iron

  Option: vinegar

METHOD

1. Cut fabric into sizes as required for each student. Students may also bring in an old white t-shirt they want to decorate.

2. Cut flowers from stems, being sure to leave some of the stem attached. Leaves can be left in small clusters, rather than individual ones. Students may choose to have many different leaf types and shapes.

3. As students will be pounding with a hammer, they need to work on a solid floor or a sturdy bench. Cover the surface with a layer of cardboard.

4. Arrange leaves and/or flowers on fabric. Use small pieces of masking tape to pin these flat on material. Use more masking tape to cover the whole leaf or flower.

5. Turn the fabric over. With safety glasses on, students can use the rubber mallet to hammer through the fabric and transfer the plant pigment. Make sure they pound along the edges of the plants to define the shape. Thicker flowers may require a bit more effort to transfer the pigment.

6. Turn the fabric over and peel off the masking tape and pounded leaf. Students may add more flowers to create more intricate prints.

7. Wash fabric in cold water and iron it. This helps to fix the colour. Alternatively, you can soak the fabric in vinegar for half an hour to help fix the colours. This works well for green chlorophyll prints. If mordants (alum etc.) are available, have students soak their fabrics in a solution for a few hours, then allow to dry.

PROJECT

SUN-BREWED PRINTS

MATERIALS

- ☑ large glass jars (e.g. 1 kg coffee jars, mason jars, kilner jars) and lids
- ☑ water
- ☑ kitchen strainer
- ☑ alum or cream of tartar solution (use ratio of a teaspoon of mordant to 1 litre water)

METHOD

1. Collect plant parts and either crush or chop finely, place them in the jars, and fill with water. Place a lid on the jars.

2. Leave the jars in a warm place that gets plenty of sun. After a few days, strain the colourful liquid using a kitchen strainer.

3. Add some white material or wool to the jars, and pour the coloured water back in. Top up with alum solution, replace the lids and return jars to a sunny spot for a further one to four days.

4. Remove material and rinse in cold water. Place it on paper towels to dry. Larger pieces of material can be pegged to a line.

Continued...

PROJECT

HEATED BATH

MATERIALS

- ☑ large metal pot and lid
- ☑ stove or camp cooker
- ☑ kitchen strainer
- ☑ wooden spoon
- ☑ alum or cream of tartar solution (use ratio of a teaspoon of mordant to 1 l water)

METHOD

1. Collect plant parts and either crush or chop finely, place them in the pot, cover with water and simmer for around one hour on the stove.
2. Strain the coloured liquid to remove the plant material.
3. Return the dye water to the pot. Place material in pot and use a wooden spoon to stir dye water over fabric. Students can also try 'tie dyeing' by tying knots in the material, or bunching parts of the material together using rubber bands. This will create some interesting patterns.
4. Add one cup of alum solution and simmer on the stove for an hour. Stir occasionally to see if fabric is absorbing the dye.
5. Allow to cool and remove fabric. Rinse in cold water and hang on a line to dry.

PART 4

APPENDIX
PLANTING GUIDE

It is recommended that your school have two growing periods over the course of the year. Start your winter vegetable crop in mid-autumn when it is cooler, perhaps after some rain. Plant the summer crop in late winter or early spring so as to enable some harvesting before the holidays. Be mindful that there may be some overlap – some winter vegetables may still need to be harvested while you are planting for summer.

PERENNIALS AND ANNUALS

Perennials are vegetables that can be left to grow over several years. Examples include asparagus, capsicum, eggplant and artichokes. Annuals are plants that complete their life cycle within a single growing season. After producing seeds, the plant will die. Perennials are less common than annuals, and many perennials are grown and harvested as annuals, including potatoes, kale, cherry tomatoes, garlic and brussels sprouts.

APPENDIX – PLANTING GUIDE

Vegetables and garden salad fruits for winter (plant April–May)

VEGETABLE	NOTES
BEAN *Phaseolus vulgaris*	Beans need protection from cold and wind. Grow as runners producing edible pods which can be eaten straight off the plant or cooked. Dwarf or bush varieties also available. Frost resistant but drought tender.
BEETROOT *Beta vulgaris*	Deep purple swollen root which can be boiled, roasted or eaten raw. Seeds can take some time to germinate, and germination can be inconsistent. Leaves are also edible and can be added to salads.
BOK CHOY *Brassica rapa*	Enjoys full sun. Plant with mint or salad greens.
BROCCOLI *Brassica oleracea*	Likes rich soil and full sun. Pick heads off as they mature, leaving the plant to produce more heads. To ensure a long, productive season, broccoli heads must not be allowed to flower. Grows well with dill, celery, sage and rosemary.
CABBAGE *Brassica oleracea*	Different heirloom varieties are available. Savoy cabbage is generally hardy and milder in flavour than white cabbage. Grows well with potatoes, beetroot, onions and sage.
CELERY *Apium graveolens*	Prefers a temperate or cool climate.
CHIVES *Allium schoenoprasum*	A perennial consisting of green, hollow leaves with pink flowers. Often used to flavour soups, salads and salad dressings.
GLOBE ARTICHOKE *Cynara scolymus*	Attractive vegetable grows up to 2 metres high with numerous branches. Edible stems and flowers can also be used for dried arrangements.
JAPANESE MUSTARD Mizuna – *Brassica junicea* 'Japonica'	Fern-like leaves have a sweet taste with a hint of mustard. Harvest year round leaf by leaf. Use leaves to add texture to salad.
KALE *Sinapsis arvensis*	Frost resistant but drought tender. Edible leaves. Many different varieties now available, some become perennial in mild conditions.
LEEK *Allium ampeloprasum*	Doesn't produce a bulb but a long cylinder of bundled leaf sheaths. Commonly used in soups, sliced leek sections can be eaten raw or fried. While it takes six months to fully mature it can be picked and used young.

Continued...

APPENDIX – PLANTING GUIDE

VEGETABLE	NOTES
LETTUCE *Lactuca sativa*	Prefers open sandy or loamy soil in a partly shaded area, as the hot sun will wilt leaves. Fully grown in eight to 12 weeks. You may be able to plant a 'repeat lettuce', which doesn't produce a head but does provide the option of just picking a number of (outer) leaves as needed. Grows well with strawberries, onions and cabbage.
ONION *Allium cepa*	Bulb of swollen leaves, commonly used in fried dishes, salads, pickles and chutneys. Can be picked young, but most often harvested when green leaves die back and the outer scales of the bulbs dry.
PARSNIP *Pastinaca sativa*	A root vegetable, related to carrots and parsley, it is often used in stews, roasts, soups and casseroles. As it matures it becomes sweeter, but will turn woodier if left too long in the ground.
PEAS *Pisum sativum*	A green climbing annual (needs staking/trellis). Some varieties are considered tastier than others, so try a few varieties and see what works best for your soil and climate. Grows well with carrots, radish and beans.
POTATO *Solanum tuberosum*	Produces a spring and autumn root crop. Does not like frost, and hot weather can sometimes reduce crops as it will go to seed. Grown in stacked-up tyres or strawbales will provide an ample crop. Green potatoes are poisonous.
RADISH *Raphanus raphanistrum* subsp. *sativus*	Crunchy salad vegetable, with a sharp flavour. Seeds germinate quickly and grows fast, reaching maturity in about four weeks. Both the leaves and swollen root are edible. Good companion plant and that seems unaffected by disease and pests.
ROCKET *Eruca vesicaria* spp. *sativa*	Fast growing salad herb. Leaves are mild when grown in winter with lots of watering, but can have a peppery flavour in warmer weather or if they lack water. Requires rich soil conditions.
SILVER BEET *Beta vulgaris*	Biennial vegetable. Height approximately 70 centimetres. Pale celery coloured stalks and dark green leaves, both edible. Leaves grow back when harvested.
SPINACH (ENGLISH) *Spinacea olearacea*	An annual that quickly goes to seed. Leaves can be eaten raw or cooked. Grows well with broad beans, strawberries and fruit trees.
SWEET POTATO *Ipomoea batatas*	Sweet potato has edible tubers and edible (young) leaves that can be cooked like spinach. It is a perennial groundcover (can also trail/climb) and serves as a weed suppressant and fire-retardant. Easy to grow from cuttings (slips) or from sprouted 'eyes' on tubers.
TURNIP *Brassica rapa* subsp. *rapa*	A white-coloured root vegetable, its boiled leaves are also edible. A yellow-fleshed variety is sometimes called a swede.

APPENDIX – PLANTING GUIDE

Vegetables and garden salad fruits for summer (plant in August)

VEGETABLE	NOTES
ASPARAGUS *Asparagus officinalis*	Male and female perennial plants, which can grow for up to 20 years. Male plants produce fat spears, remain permanently where planted, prefer to be grown alone but can companion plant with parsley and tomatoes. Fruits late winter, early spring. Frost tolerant, prefers full sun.
CHILLI ROCOTILLO *Capsicum frutescents*	A biennial, green-leafed, small shrub. Edible, hot red fruit. Height to 50 centimetres.
CAPE GOOSEBERRY OR CHINESE LANTERN *Physalis alkikengi*	A perennial shrub growing to 1 metre. Edible fruit, good foliage for mulch and poultry feed. The fruit is a round yellow berry 2 centimetres in diameter, quite sweet when fully ripe and tart when under ripe. The fruit is enclosed in its own lantern or husk which protects it from insects. The husk turns from green to yellow, and soon after the berry changes from green to a deep golden yellow. Prune severely after fruiting. Plants can be staked but self-support easily.
CAPSICUM PEPPERS *Capsicum annum*	Frost tender. Grow in an open, sunny, well-drained position out of the wind. Fruit can be yellow, red or green.
CARROTS *Daucus carota*	Sweet root vegetable. Grows well with leeks, lettuce, peas and tomatoes. Growing it in sandy soil produces straighter roots.
CEYLON SPINACH *Basella alba*	Ceylon or Malabar spinach is an edible perennial vine. It may be used to thicken soups. The leaves are used in stir fries.
CHERRY TOMATO *Lycoperiscon pimpinellifolium*	Often perennial, with fruit production over a long period, the cherry tomato likes a sunny location and will require staking or growing on a trellis. The fruit is sweet and flavoursome and the bite-sized portions make them perfect for snacking and appealing to children.
CHILLI *Capsicum annum*	Is a perennial plant, often grown as an annual in the tropics. Not frost hardy. Can be sundried, shredded and chopped in cooking for a hot spicy flavour.

Continued...

APPENDIX – PLANTING GUIDE

VEGETABLE	NOTES
CUCUMBER *Cucumis sativus*	Requires fertile soil. Can be grown as a trellis crop or over the ground.
EGGPLANT (AUBERGINE) *Solanum melengena*	A perennial bush to 0.6 metres grown as an annual with long, grey-green toothed leaves. It is frost tender and prefers a well-drained sandy loam. It has large purple egg-shaped fruit which are edible when ripe and cooked.
PUMPKIN *Cucurbita spp.*	General purpose vegetable. Grows on a vine and can grow over objects such as sheds for insulation or up trees to save space. Needs fertile soil and good amounts of water. Grows well with sweetcorn. Susceptible to powdery mildew when watered from above.
RHUBARB *Rheum rhabarbum*	Edible green or red stalks. Leaves are high in oxalic acid and can be fermented and used as an insect repellent.
ROCKMELON *Cucumis melon*	Sprawling vine with large edible fruit. Grow in sunny position, in a well-drained mound of well-rotted compost or manure.
SWEET CORN *Zea mays*	An annual plant to 2 metres. Prefers an open, sunny position with plenty of water. Edible cobs are bright yellow. Eat fresh, as they do not store for long periods.
TOMATO *Lycopersicon esculentum*	Salad vegetable grows upright and likes a sunny position. Excellent source of vitamins A and C. Needs to be staked as it grows. Can attain a height of over 2 metres. Fruit is picked as it ripens to red colour. Can be eaten fresh, used in sauces, soups and hot dishes or preserved green as pickles. Freeze only after cooking. Grows well with basil, carrots, lima beans and asparagus. The leaves can be used as an insect repellent.
ZUCCHINI *Cucurbita pepo*	Zucchini is a dark or light green vegetable, which is usually cooked and presented as a savoury dish or accompaniment. Zucchini flowers can also be fried and eaten.

APPENDIX – PLANTING GUIDE

HERBS

HERBS FOR COOKING

The oils and other aromatic chemicals in the leaves and flowers of herbs provide seasoning and flavours to food. When other parts of plants are used (such as the seeds, bark or root), we call them spices. Spices include turmeric, cinnamon, ginger, cloves, galangal and nutmeg.

HERB	NOTES
CORIANDER *Coriandrum sativum*	This is an annual herb growing to about 50 centimetres tall. Fresh leaves are added to chutneys, salads and curries, and often as a garnish on cooked food. The crushed root is used in Thai cuisine. The leaves contain high amounts of vitamins K, C, A and E (in this order) and reasonable amounts of the minerals iron, manganese and potassium. The seeds (dry fruits) can be used whole or ground to a powder, and this spice adds an aromatic, citrus flavour to many dishes. Coriander leaf is also called cilantro.
PARSLEY *Petroselinum crispum*	Parsley is high in vitamins A, C and K and is a common garnish for salads, meat and potato dishes, and soups. The curly-leaf variety (var. *crispum*) is more decorative than the flat-leaf variety (Italian, var. *neapolitanum*), but both are easy to grow from seed. In cooler climates parsley may be biennial but in warmer climates it tends to be an annual.
THYME *Thymus* spp.	The tiny leaves of many thyme species are added as seasoning to omelettes or scrambled eggs and a variety of meats and sauces. Like rosemary, finely-chopped or dried thyme leaves can be sprinkled onto bread dough to make a savoury loaf. For a mild citrus flavour use lemon thyme (*Thymus citriodorus*). The leaves do not contain many nutrients, but do contain an aromatic compound called thymol that is a good antiseptic and gives thyme its strong flavour.
LEMON BALM *Melissa officinalis*	Lemon balm is a bushy, hardy, herbaceous perennial to 1 metre that tolerates shade. The small white flowers attract bees. Use the leaves as a flavouring to fish and poultry dishes, or add in salads. Herbal tea made from an infusion of the leaves is known to reduce stress and have a calming effect.
LEMONGRASS *Cymbopogon citratus*	A perennial grass that has dense clumps of long, tapered leaves, which are used in teas and Asian cooking. Common in tropical regions, but can be grown in other climatic zones provided it receives adequate water and shelter, especially from frosts. Plant where it can be well-watered.
LEMON VERBENA *Aloysia citriodora* (syn. *A. triphylla*)	An evergreen shrub in warm, humid climates but can be deciduous in colder climates. The leaves are used to add a lemon fragrance to cooking or herbal teas. Popular in fragrant herb mixes for potpourri or sleep pillows. Trim after it flowers each year to maintain its bushiness and prevent it from becoming scraggly.

APPENDIX – PLANTING GUIDE

PEST-REPELLENT HERBS

Many herbs contain oils and other chemicals that repel pests. Pest control is not only about repelling pests, it is also about attracting predators into the garden.

HERB	NOTES
SCENTED PELARGONIUMS *Pelargonium* spp.	There is a wide variety of scented pelargoniums available. They are all good, general pest repellents as pests are deterred by the strong smell of their leaves. Some pelargoniums can also be used in herbal teas and to add flavour in cooking. Pelargoniums grow best in well-drained, fertile soil in full sun but can withstand dry conditions quite well. The leaves from various lemon-scented pelargoniums (containing citronella oil) can be rubbed on the skin to deter mosquitoes. Pelargoniums are often incorrectly called geraniums, but while the two types of plants are related they are distinctly different.
SANTOLINA OR COTTON LAVENDER *Santolina chamaecyparissus* or *S. incana*	Santolina is an attractive, compact, small shrub with grey foliage and yellow button-like flowers. It prefers well-drained soil, tolerates full sun and is drought hardy. The leaves are used to repel moths (in clothing drawers and pantry shelves). Both the leaves (fresh or dried) and sprigs are suitable.

APPENDIX – PLANTING GUIDE

NATIVE PLANTS

For thousands of years, Indigenous Australians made use of Australia's flora. They soon learned which plants were edible and how each fruit, nut, root, stem or leaf had to be prepared and treated for safe consumption. Many plants were also used as bush medicine, and research into the active ingredients of these plants have yielded promising results.

The availability of these plants may sometimes be seasonal, and many are only available in some states and at some specialist nurseries. This is a generic list of species found in different regions of Australia. You may find that many may not grow in your climate and soil. Seek advice from your local nursery.

PLANT	NOTES
AUSTRALIAN OR WA BLUEBELL *Billardiera heterophylla* (formerly *Sollya heterophylla*)	A shrub up to 1.5 metres high with stems that twine around themselves and other plants. The leathery leaves are up to 5 centimetres long. The flowers possess blue petals and the edible fruit that is produced can be up to 2.5 centimetres long with many seeds embedded in the pulp. Flowers October to February.
BROWN PINE *Podocarpus elatus*	Evergreen, medium tree, usually less than 10 metres in cultivation. Leaves oblong, dark green to 10 centimetres. Edible fruit purplish-black to 25 millimetres diameter. Tolerant of mild frosts but needs summer watering. Fruit can be eaten raw or made into jam.
BRUSH OR SCRUB CHERRY *Syzygium australe*	Medium tree which produces pink to red fruit about 2 centimetres long. The round seed is easily removed and the tart pulp makes an excellent jam.
BURDEKIN PLUM *Pleiogynium timorense*	Tree to 4–5 metres. Large purple-black fruit, with thin, apricot-flavoured flesh around a large stone. Can be used in sauces, to make wine and whole plum can be pickled in vinegar. Separate male and female flowers. Fruit normally kept a few days to soften them and make palatable.
DAVIDSON'S PLUM *Davidsonia* spp.	*Davidsonia* is a genus containing three rainforest tree species, each producing an edible sour fruit with red-purple coloured flesh. They are small trees to about 5 metres (*Davidsonia jerseyana*, and *Davidsonia johnsonii*), but *Davidsonia pruriens* can be taller. The fruit is found in clusters on the stem.
EMU PLUM OR KEROSENE BUSH *Podocarpus drouynianus*	A large bushy shrub from the south-west of WA to 2.5 metres, prefers shade and the large attractive foliage is used for cut flower arrangements. The fruit is purple/dark blue in colour and is up to 4 centimetres length. One end contains the seed part (green) which is discarded and the fleshy 'fruit' (about the size of a grape) is eaten. What is eaten is actually the fleshy stalk of the true fruit. Male and female plants.
FINGER LIME *Citrus australasica*	Finger limes naturally occur in rainforests in southern Queensland and northern New South Wales. The skin and flesh can vary in colour due to breeding by nurseries. Leaves are much smaller than common citrus types.

APPENDIX – PLANTING GUIDE

PLANT	NOTES
FLAX LILY *Dianella revoluta variegata*	This variety possesses evergreen, blue-green leaves with striking cream edges to 0.5 metres. Blue flowers and purple berry fruit are arranged on a tall (1 metre) spike. Tolerant of most soils and climate conditions. The fruit can be eaten raw, the roots can be pounded, roasted and then eaten while the leaves are used to make string and cord. Dianella is also a waterwise native.
KURRAJONG *Brachychiton* spp.	There are about thirty species of kurrajong or bottle trees. They grow from 4 metres to over 20 metres tall and, while most are evergreen, some are dry season deciduous. Like many Australian native plants, kurrajongs had many uses in Aboriginal culture, including eating the roasted seeds, using the wood to make shields and using the bark as fibre and for fishing lines. The leaves are stock fodder.
LEMON ASPEN *Acronychia acidula*	Lemon aspen is a medium-sized rainforest tree from northern Queensland. The aromatic and acidic fruit is harvested to add a tart lemon flavour to foods.
LEMON-SCENTED MYRTLE *Backhousia citriodora*	Bushy small to medium tree with dark green lemon-scented leaves. Leaves are used fresh or dried and ground to make tea, or are added to cakes, sauces and meat dishes. Leaves contain the lemon-lime oil 'Citral'.
LILLY PILLY *Syzgium smithii* (formerly *Acmena smithii*)	Lilly pilly is the common name for several species, all with similar pink-red fruit. They are evergreen rainforest trees with glossy green leaves, but new nursery varieties can be bought with brown or pink tips. Some varieties are also dwarf and compact and are used as hedge plants in landscaping.
MACADAMIA *Macadamia integrifolia* and *M. tetraphylla*	Macadamia is Australia's only commercial nut tree. The nuts are eaten raw or after cooking. These seeds have high energy and fat content. Macadamias prefer a warm subtropical climate and a well-drained soil. These trees are slow growing.
MAROON OR CURRANT BUSH *Scaevola spinescens*	Drought and frost resistant, prefers dry and well-drained soils. Height 1 metre and 1 metre spread. White flowers, with purple streaks appearing in autumn and spring. Important plant in Aboriginal culture. They burned this plant and inhaled the smoke as a treatment for colds. Edible blue-purple berries, and has other medical properties.
MIDYIM BERRY *Austromyrtus dulcis*	Small shrub that grows to half a metre in height. New leaves have a pink tinge, and the flowers are white. The small, pea-sized berries are edible and are white with purple spots.
MOUNTAIN PEPPER *Tasmannia lanceolata*	Mountain pepper is a small shrub found in south-eastern Australia. There are separate male and female plants. The leaves and berries have a strong pepper flavour.

APPENDIX – PLANTING GUIDE

PLANT	NOTES
MUNTRIES OR MUNTARI *Kunzea pomifera*	Low-lying shrub from the eastern states, useful ground cover with white flowers and small edible fruit (apple-like). It prefers a well-drained soil and is found spreading over sand or rocks. The fruit is found on the underside of the shrub.
NATIVE GINGER *Alpinia caerulea*	Leaf shoots and berries have a mild ginger flavour. Can be eaten fresh or used in cooking. A strap-like clumping plant, it prefers semi-shade, and will suffer if placed in full sun.
PERSOONIA *Persoonia* spp.	There are many species of *Persoonia* throughout Australia, and they are mostly shrubs or small trees. They are often called Snottygobble in WA and SA, and Geebung in the eastern states. Some regions refer to them as native olives because the fruit starts as green and turns black with age. It has one central seed like an olive. Not all fruits seem to be palatable.
QUANDONG OR NATIVE PEACH *Santalum acuminatum*	A small parasitic tree to four metres. The fruit are shiny red when ripe and about the size of a thumbnail. The flesh has a yellow colour. The large pitted nut occupies much of the fruit and has to be cracked to extract the kernel which is eaten raw. Oil from the seeds is used for cosmetic purposes. The kernel is high in energy, protein and fat while the fleshy fruit is high in water and carbohydrates. Fruit used to make jam.
RASPBERRY JAM WATTLE *Acacia acuminata*	A small tree up to 6 metres. Seeds are collected and ground into flour, mixed with water and cooked as small cakes in the coals of a fire. Gum from wattles is also edible and often mixed with water to make a weak tea. This is one of the host plants for quandong and sandalwood. A Waterwise native plant.
RIBERRY *Syzygium luemanni*	Small pink berries, to 2 centimetres diameter, with a cinnamon and clove taste. Medium tree 6–10 metres. prefers sunny position. Fruit can be eaten raw or used in jams, sauces, to flavour ice-cream and to make soft drinks. Many species of *Syzygium* are available at nurseries.
ROUND LIME *Citrus australis*	A small tree naturally occurring in southeast Queensland. It produces round fruit with a thick skin and pale green pulp. Leaves are small.
SAMPHIRE *Tecticornia* spp. (e.g. *T. pergranulata*)	Native succulents found in waterlogged soil and salty flats. Leaves can be eaten raw, but also blanched. Crunchy in texture, the leaves add a salt and slight aromatic flavour to dishes.

APPENDIX – PLANTING GUIDE

PLANT	NOTES
SANDALWOOD OR BUSH PLUM *Santalum lanceolatum* and *S. spicatum*	A small tree up to 6 metres high. The leaves are fleshy, bluish in colour and oval in shape. The yellow-white flowers grow in clusters and the fruit produced vary from brown to purple or black when mature. The bark is used as a bush medicine. Both *Santalum lanceolatum* and *S. spicatum* are known as sandalwood. The leaves and wood can be burnt to repel mosquitoes.
SMALL-LEAF TAMARIND *Diploglottis campbelli*	Small evergreen tree to 7–8 metres. The fruit capsule often contains three bright red-coated seeds. The red, thin flesh around the seed is edible, and is acid to taste. Its tangy flavour has sweet and savoury applications. It can be made into jams, jellies, drinks, chutneys and sauces. This tree is endangered in its native habitat in northern NSW.
WARRIGAL GREENS OR NEW ZEALAND SPINACH *Tetragonia tetragonioides*	While young leaves can be eaten raw in salads, it is best to boil the leaves and then discard the water, as the leaves contain oxalic acid. Warrigal greens is very hardy and is tolerant of drought, infertile soil and salinity.
WEEPING PITTOSPORUM OR NATIVE APRICOT *Pittosporum angustifolium* (formerly *Pittosporum phillyreoides*)	A small tree from the central desert which grows to 6 metres. The gum in branches is eaten and it is rich in carbohydrates. The fruits are orange and about 2 centimetres, oval in shape. The seed can be ground to make an oily paste which is used as bush medicine and rubbed on sore areas of the body. The red seeds are poisonous.

APPENDIX – PLANTING GUIDE

BUSH MEDICINE PLANTS

There are many native plants used as bush medicines by Indigenous Australians throughout Australia. The ones listed here are some of the more common ones that you may be able to obtain from nurseries. It is a worthwhile project to have some part of the garden planted out with indigenous plants of cultural significance.

PLANT	NOTES
BLOODROOT *Haemodorum* spp.	Used to cure dysentery. The roots are eaten raw or roasted with a spicy, onion-like flavour. The bulb-like leaf bases are roasted, pounded together with clay from termite nests and eaten.
BROAD LEAF PAPERBARK *Melaleuca quinquenervia*	Medium-sized tree with yellow-green flowers. Drought tolerant and survives in waterlogged soils. Useful windbreak and bird-attracting. The oil of this paperbark contains menthol compounds. The leaves are pulverised and the volatile compounds are inhaled to clear blocked sinuses and airways. The bark of many paperbarks is used as bandages.
CAMPHOR MYRTLE *Babingtonia camphorosmae* (formerly *Baeckea camphorosmae*)	Used to treat headaches, by waving the crushed leaves under the nose of the sufferer.
HOP BUSH *Dodonea viscosa/purpurea*	Erect, bushy shrub, 3 metres high, 1.5 metre in diameter. Infusion used to sponge the body to relieve fever. Boiled root or juice applied for toothache. A hardy plant which tolerates drought, pollution and coastal, salty winds.
KANGAROO APPLE *Solanum laciniatum* and also known as *Solanum aviculare*	Bright purple flowers that produce egg-like fruits that ripen to an orange or red colour. The fruit can be eaten, but can also be used as part of a poultice to treat swollen joints.
KURRAJONG *Brachychiton diversifolium*	Large tree from central Australia. The inner bark is crushed in water and the resulting solution is used as an eyewash.
LEAFLESS BALLART *Exocarpos aphyllus*	A decoction of mashed stems is taken for colds and used to wash sores. Also used as a poultice on the chest for 'wasting diseases'.
LEMON SCENTED GUM *Corymbia citriodora*	Large tree, with scented leaves and spreading branches. The gum is an antibiotic and contains citriodoral.
MAROON OR CURRANT BUSH *Scaevola spinescens*	Drought and frost resistant, prefers dry and well-drained soils. Height 1 metre and 1 metre spread. White flowers, with purple streaks appearing in autumn and spring. Aborigines burned this plant and inhaled the smoke as a treatment for colds. Edible berries, and has other medical properties.

APPENDIX – PLANTING GUIDE

PLANT	NOTES
NATIVE LEMON GRASS *Cymbopogon ambiguus*	The plant is cut up, boiled in water and the resulting liquid used to bathe the body for general illness. Small quantities can be drunk as a treatment for a sore throat.
OLD MAN SALTBUSH *Atriplex nummularia*	The leaves can be steamed or boiled to create a treatment to bathe skin sores, burns and wounds.
PIG FACE *Carpobrotus* spp.	Pig face is a valuable food plant. The centre of the red or purple berry is a sweet tasty fruit. The leaves were cooked and eaten. The juice from the leaves was used to soothe blisters, burns and pain from insect bites, and applied to stings from jellyfish.
RED RIVER GUM *Eucalyptus camaldulensis*	Large tree which prefers wet areas. The gum is dissolved in water and the solution drunk to relieve diarrhoea.
SANDPAPER FIG *Ficus opposita*	The rough leaves have been used to treat fungal infections such as ringworm, sometimes in combination with the sap.
SPOTTED EMU BUSH (NATIVE FUCHSIA) *Eremophila maculata*	Shrub growing from 0.5 to 1 metre. Used for the treatment of colds. The leaves are boiled in water for drinking or rubbed on the body.
TEA TREE *Melaleuca alternifolia*	Tea-tree oil has proven antiseptic potency and has been used to treat common skin ailments and fungal infections.
WATTLE *Acacia* spp.	Usually small shrubs to medium-sized trees, scattered throughout Australia. Bark is used for skin conditions such as boils. Bark and gum eaten for diarrhoea. The thorns of some prickly species such as *A. farnesiana*, *A. pulchella* and *A. victoriae* are used to remove splinters.
WEEPING PITTOSPORUM OR NATIVE APRICOT *Pittosporum angustifolium* (formerly *Pittosporum phillyreoides*)	A small tree from the central desert which grows to 6 metres. The gum in branches is eaten and it is rich in carbohydrates. The fruits are orange and about 2 centimetres, oval in shape. The seed can be ground to make an oily paste which is used as bush medicine and rubbed on sore areas of the body. The red seeds are poisonous.
WHITE CASCADE *Sannantha bidwillii*	A shrub growing to 1 metre tall and displaying weeping foliage. Prefers a well-drained, fertile soil in full sun. Drought tolerant once stabilised. Ideal for rockeries and waterwise gardens. Some species of *Sannantha* and similar species are used as bush medicine.

APPENDIX – PLANTING GUIDE

PLANTS FOR ATTRACTING BUTTERFLIES

Butterflies are important pollinators. Both native plants and common exotics in our gardens attract butterflies. While specific species are mentioned below, you may be able to find local species of the same genus that may be suitable too. Some plants provide food, such as nectar from their flowers, some plants are hosts for the butterfly larvae, and some plants provide shelter and habitat.

PLANT	NOTES
BERRY SALTBUSH *Rhagodia baccata* (syn. *Chenopodium baccatum*)	Spreading shrub 2 metres high and wide. Coastal, tough plant. Red berries follow flowering in early winter. Fruit is edible but slightly bitter, and is preferred by lizards and birds. Leaves can be cooked and eaten. Saltbush Blue butterflies breed in this plant.
BUTTERFLY PLANT *Buddleja davidii* (also spelt *Buddleia*)	Deciduous tall shrub to about 3 metres, with mauve flowers. Hardy, low maintenance, although annual pruning is recommended to keep a compact shape. Butterflies love this plant, but they do prefer purple colour over white or some of the other varieties.
CREEPING SALTBUSH *Atriplex semibaccata*	Small shrub that is tolerant of dry and saline conditions. Edible fruits, and is used as animal fodder and erosion control on farms. The Saltbush Blue butterfly uses this plant – for nectar and as a host plant for the butterfly larvae.
FLAX LILY *Dianella revoluta*	Evergreen, blue-green leaves, blue flowers and purple berry fruit which are arranged on a tall (1 metre) spike. Tolerant of most soils and climate conditions. The fruit can be eaten raw, the roots can be pounded, roasted and then eaten while the leaves are used to make string and cord. Many native grasses provide habitat for many butterflies, such as the Wedge grass-skipper, Western grass-dirt and Common brown.
GOLDEN WREATH WATTLE *Acacia saligna*	Large-leaved wattle from the south-west of WA. Good fodder for sheep, goats, horses and cattle. Fast-growing, fire retardant, nitrogen-fixing shrub to 4 metres. It is suitable for soil stabilisation, does well in coastal areas and is ideal for wind break and erosion control. Aborigines used the seeds to make flour. The Amethyst Hairstreak, Varied Hairstreak, Two-spotted Line-blue and Wattle Blue butterflies frequent this plant.
GREEN STINKWOOD *Jacksonia sternbergiana*	Shrub to a few metres with yellow and orange flowers. Weeping habit and reduced leaves as adaptations to drought. Provides food for the larvae of several species of butterfly. Like the golden wreath wattle, stinkwood is the host for many insects.
KANGAROO APPLE *Solanum laciniatum* and also known as *Solanum aviculare*	These species are very similar and difficult to tell apart. Fast growing shrubs to 3 metres. Butterflies obtain nectar from this plant.

Continued...

APPENDIX – PLANTING GUIDE

PLANT	NOTES
KURRAJONG *Brachychiton populneus*	Good shade tree with glossy-green foliage which is useful stock fodder. Ground-up seeds can be brewed as a coffee substitute (burn or rub off irritating hairs first). Swollen taproot is nutritious and can be eaten. Gum is also edible. Host for the Pencilled Blue.
NATIVE MINT BUSH *Prostanthera sieberi*	Compact small shrub to about 1 metre. Mauve flowers and mint-scented leaves. Tolerates wide range of soils (coastal sands to clays), climates and light from full sun to partial shade. Attracts butterflies and small insect-eating birds. Drought hardy and frost tolerant once established.
PINK RICE FLOWER *Pimelea ferruginea*	Small shrub to 1 metre high and spread, pink flowers in spring and tolerant of a wide range of soils, drought and partial shade. Endemic to the south-west of WA. Nectar source for adult butterflies.
QUANDONG OR NATIVE PEACH *Santalum acuminatum*	A small parasitic tree to 4 metres. The fruit are red when ripe and the flesh has a yellow colour. The large pitted nut occupies much of the fruit and has to be cracked to extract the kernel which is eaten raw. Oil from the seeds is used for cosmetic purposes. The kernel is high in energy, protein and fat, while the fleshy fruit is high in carbohydrates and used to make jam. The large Spotted Jezebel butterfly feeds on this plant.
RASPBERRY JAM WATTLE *Acacia acuminata*	A small tree up to 6 metres. Seeds are collected and ground into flour, mixed with water and cooked as small cake in the coals of a fire. Gum from wattles is also edible and often mixed with water to make a weak tea. This is one of the host plants for Quandong and Sandalwood. The Amethyst Hairstreak butterfly frequents this plant.
SANDALWOOD OR BUSH PLUM *Santalum spicatum*	A small tree up to 6 metres high. The leaves are fleshy, bluish in colour and oval in shape. The yellow-white flowers grow in clusters and the fruit produced vary from red to purple or black when mature. The sweet fruit can be eaten raw. The bark is used as a bush medicine. The leaves and wood can be burnt to repel mosquitoes. The Spotted Jezebel butterfly feeds on this plant.
TROPICAL MILKWEED *Asclepias curassavica*	Easy-to-grow shrub to about 1.5 metres, with yellow to red flowers (also known as Bloodflower). In cold climates it can be an annual but in warmer areas tends to become perennial for at least a few years. Originally from South America, it is naturalised throughout the world as it is a well-known host for Monarch butterflies. In WA it is also the host for the local Lesser Wanderer.
WOOLLY DAISY BUSH *Olearia languinosa*	A tough, hardy plant with grey foliage that grows in full sun. Produces small daisy-like flowers in spring through to autumn. Low, spreading shrub. The Australian Painted Lady prefers plants of the daisy family which are rich sources of nectar.

APPENDIX – PLANTING GUIDE

PLANTS FOR ATTRACTING OTHER BENEFICIAL INSECTS

Beneficial insects are those that may be essential for pollination or they predate on pests and weeds. Beneficials include bees, hoverflies, parasitic wasps, green lacewings, assassin bugs and ladybirds. Plants can provide food or habitat.

Many of these plants are common herbs, but a few are a little harder to source. Most self-propagate with abundant seed or through cuttings and rhizomes.

PLANT	NOTES
BASKET OF GOLD *Alyssum saxatillis*	Small evergreen perennial that produces yellow flowers in spring. Ideal for rock or dry garden areas, provided the drainage is good. This ground cover has fine shivery leaves and is a useful nectar plant. Attracts hoverflies and ladybirds.
BLUE THIMBLE FLOWER *Gilia capitata*	Small annual shrub to 40 centimetres, with blue flowers and soft, bushy foliage. Drought tolerant and prefers sunny position. Self-seeds so you will get plants year after year.
BORAGE *Borago officinalis*	Small shrub to 80 centimetres. Leaves are useful in compost or to make liquid fertiliser. Blue flowers are edible, good bee forage. Young leaves are also used in salads, but older larger leaves tend to be hairy.
CORIANDER *Coriandrum sativum*	Seeds are essential for tomato chutney and curries, and they can be added to soups and sauces. The leaves are used in salads and poultry dishes. Has a reputation of repelling aphids and other sap suckers.
DILL *Anethum graveolens*	Dill is an annual herb that is used as a spice for flavouring food. Dill oil (from the leaves, stems and seeds) is used in the manufacturing of soaps. Dill attracts many beneficial insects (such as hoverflies, lacewings and parasitic wasps) as the umbrella flower heads go to seed.
FALSE QUEEN ANNE'S LACE *Ammi majus*	Annual plant with small white flower heads. Grows in full or part sun to 1 metre high and 40 centimetres wide. Self-seeds readily so you will always have plants.
FENNEL *Foeniculum vulgare*	One of the oldest cultivated herbs which readily self-seeds. Flowering fennel attracts an enormous range of predators and also repels fleas and other pests.
HYSSOP *Hyssopus officinalis*	Small shrub to 60 centimetres, produces masses of pink to blue fragrant flowers, resistant to drought and thrives in full sun. Historical use as a medicinal plant. Bees make a rich and aromatic honey from the flowers. Attracts beneficial wasps.

Continued...

APPENDIX – PLANTING GUIDE

PLANT	NOTES
LACY PHACELIA *Phacelia tanacetifolia*	Annual plant to 1 metre. Nectar-rich purple-blue flowers that attract hoverflies. Fern-like lobed leaves, prefers sunny position, can be used as a green manure crop.
QUEEN ANNE'S LACE *Daucus carota*	Flowers in late spring to late autumn with large white flower heads. Attracts hoverflies, lacewings and parasitic wasps. A biennial plant. 1 metre high and 50 centimetres wide. Self-seeds readily so you may want to cut some seed heads off to stop extensive spread.
SWEET ALYSSUM *Lobularia maritima* (syn. *Alyssum maritimum*)	Drought hardy, low-lying annual plant that produces white fragrant flowers. It self-sows so new plants pop up each year.
TANSY *Tanacetum vulgare*	Used as a repellent to keep mice, flies, fleas and ants at bay, but also attracts lacewings and ladybirds. This plant can be invasive if left unattended however.
YARROW *Achillea millefolium*	An ancient herb with vigorous, spreading root system. Leaves grow from underground rhizomes and are feathery and aromatic. Attracts many insect species, who use it as a food source.

APPENDIX – AUSTRALIAN CURRICULUM ALIGNMENT

AUSTRALIAN CURRICULUM ALIGNMENT

SCIENCE

The chart below aligns the Australian Curriculum's 'Science Understanding' strand with the investigations found in this book. You can learn more by visiting the Australian Curriculum website: https://australiancurriculum.edu.au/f-10-curriculum/science/structure/

FOUNDATION

SCIENCE UNDERSTANDING	ACTIVITIES	PAGE
BIOLOGICAL SCIENCES		
• Living things have basic needs, including food and water (ACSSU002) • Daily and seasonal changes in our environment affect everyday life (ACSSU004)	• What do plants need? • Testing soil moisture and watering plants • Evaporation	18 38 34

YEAR 1

CONTENT DESCRIPTIONS	ACTIVITIES	PAGE
BIOLOGICAL SCIENCES		
• Living things have a variety of external features (ACSSU017) • Living things live in different places where their needs are met (ACSSU211)	• Stems and leaves • What do plants need? • Earthworms in action! • What's inside a seed? • Soil particles	56 18 29 43 23

YEAR 2

CONTENT DESCRIPTIONS	ACTIVITIES	PAGE
BIOLOGICAL SCIENCES		
• Living things grow, change and have offspring similar to themselves (ACSSU30)	• What do plants need? • What's inside a seed? • Germination in a jar • Observing life cycles	18 43 52 88
EARTH AND SPACE SCIENCES		
• Earth's resources are used in a variety of ways (ACSSU032)	• Exploring the garden • Soil particles	11 23

APPENDIX — AUSTRALIAN CURRICULUM ALIGNMENT

YEAR 3

CONTENT DESCRIPTIONS	ACTIVITIES	PAGE
BIOLOGICAL SCIENCES		
• Living things can be grouped on the basis of observable features and can be distinguished from non-living things (ACSSU044)	• Fruit sorting • Design a seed	67 102

YEAR 4

CONTENT DESCRIPTIONS	ACTIVITIES	PAGE
BIOLOGICAL SCIENCES		
• Living things have life cycles (ACSSU072) • Living things depend on each other and the environment to survive (ACSSU073)	• Observing life cycles • Banana breakdown • Animal interactions simulation	88 32 92
EARTH AND SPACE SCIENCES		
• Earth's surface changes over time as a result of natural processes and human activity (ACSSU075)	• Soil particles • Soil permeability • Earthworms in action!	23 24 29

YEAR 5

CONTENT DESCRIPTIONS	ACTIVITIES	PAGE
BIOLOGICAL SCIENCES		
• Living things have structural features and adaptations that help them to survive in their environment (ACSSU043)	• Adaptations of climbing plants • Design a seed	98 102
PHYSICAL SCIENCES		
• Light from a source forms shadows and can be absorbed, reflected and refracted (ACSSU080)	• Hidden colours	111

YEAR 6

CONTENT DESCRIPTIONS	ACTIVITIES	PAGE
BIOLOGICAL SCIENCES		
• The growth and survival of living things are affected by physical conditions of their environment (ACSSU094)	• Soil particles • Soil permeability • Comparing mulches • Animal interactions simulation • Design a seed	23 24 36 92 102

APPENDIX — AUSTRALIAN CURRICULUM ALIGNMENT

DESIGN AND TECHNOLOGIES

Content from the Australian Curriculum: Design and Technologies is present throughout the activities and projects featured in this book. Some key content descriptions have been listed below along with a non-exhaustive list of corresponding activities.

YEARS F–2

CONTENT DESCRIPTIONS	EXAMPLE ACTIVITIES	PAGE
DESIGN AND TECHNOLOGIES KNOWLEDGE AND UNDERSTANDING		
• Identify how people design and produce familiar products, services and environments and consider sustainability to meet personal and local community needs (ACTDEK001) • Explore how plants and animals are grown for food, clothing and shelter and how food is selected and prepared for healthy eating (ACTDEP005)	• Exploring the garden • Harvesting garden vegetables and fruit • Testing soil moisture • Planting seeds • Resprouting vegetables • Make products from herbs • Preserving food	11 64 38 45 86 71 77
DESIGN AND TECHNOLOGIES PROCESS AND PRODUCTION SKILLS		
• Generate, develop and record design ideas through describing, drawing and modelling (ACTDEP006) • Use materials, components, tools, equipment and techniques to safely make designed solutions (ACTDEP007)	• Exploring the garden • Gardening tools	11 15

YEARS 3–4

CONTENT DESCRIPTIONS	EXAMPLE ACTIVITIES	PAGE
DESIGN AND TECHNOLOGIES KNOWLEDGE AND UNDERSTANDING		
• Recognise the role of people in design and technologies occupations and explore factors, including sustainability, that impact on the design of products, services and environments to meet community needs (ACTDEK010) • Investigate food and fibre production and food technologies used in modern and traditional societies (ACTDEK012)	• Exploring the garden • Composting • Mini hothouses • Make a bee hotel • Exploring plant dyes	11 30 53 63 113
DESIGN AND TECHNOLOGIES PROCESS AND PRODUCTION SKILLS		
• Select and use materials, components, tools, equipment and techniques and use safe work practices to make designed solutions (ACTDEP016)	• Design a seed	102

APPENDIX — AUSTRALIAN CURRICULUM ALIGNMENT

YEARS 5–6

CONTENT DESCRIPTIONS	EXAMPLE ACTIVITIES	PAGE
DESIGN AND TECHNOLOGIES KNOWLEDGE AND UNDERSTANDING		
• Examine how people in design and technologies occupations address competing considerations, including sustainability, in the design of products, services and environments for current and future use (ACTDEK019) • Investigate how and why food and fibre are produced in managed environments and prepared to enable people to grow and be healthy (ACTDEK021)	• Pest management • Make a fruit fly trap • Collecting seed from the garden • Make seed bombs • Preserving food • Recipes for excess garden produce	105 108 84 85 77 80

APPENDIX – PLANTING DIARY

PLANTING DIARY

PLANT NAME ....

PLANTED BY ....

ON ....

HEIGHT: .... **CENTIMETRES**

HEIGHT: .... **CENTIMETRES**

DATE:

DATE:

Front Page

APPENDIX - PLANTING DIARY

HEIGHT: .... CENTIMETRES

DATE:

HEIGHT: .... CENTIMETRES

DATE:

HEIGHT: .... CENTIMETRES

DATE:

HEIGHT: .... CENTIMETRES

DATE:

APPENDIX – ANSWER SHEET
ANIMAL INTERACTIONS SIMULATION ANSWERS

ROUND 1:

Species 1 and 2: No relationship

Species 1 and 3: No relationship

Species 2 and 3: Competition

Species 1 and 4: Competition

Species 2 and 4: No relationship

Species 3 and 4: No relationship

What made survival difficult during this round? Two pairs of species were in competition with each other, making it difficult to gather enough resources.

ROUND 2:

Species 1 and 2: Parisitism

Species 1 and 3: Parisitism

Species 2 and 3: Competition

Species 1 and 4: Parisitism

Species 2 and 4: Competition

Species 3 and 4: No Relationship

What made survival difficult during this round? Species 1 was able to feed on the resources of the all other species. Some other species were also in competition with each other for food.

ROUND 3:

Species 1 and 2: Mutualism

Species 1 and 3: Mutualism

Species 2 and 3: Mutualism

Species 1 and 4: Mutualism

Species 2 and 4: Mutualism

Species 3 and 4: Mutualism

How was this round different to the two previous rounds? Rather than being in competition, all species had to work together to ensure their needs were met.

ROUND 4:

Species 1 and 2: Competition

Species 1 and 3: Commensalism

Species 2 and 3: Commensalism

Species 1 and 4: Commensalism

Species 2 and 4: Commensalism

Species 3 and 4: Competition

Which species had the best chance of survival? Species 1 had the best chance. Species 3 and 4 were in competition for their only food source. Although species 1 and 2 were also in competition, species 1 could eat both blue and green food, meaning it had more food available that others could not eat.

www.ingramcontent.com/pod-product-compliance
Lightning Source LLC
Chambersburg PA
CBHW042021090526
44591CB00023B/2922